VALUES

VALUES

The Key to a Meaningful Life

A
Vedanta Kesari
Presentation

Sri Ramakrishna Math
Madras 600 004
India

Published by
The President
Sri Ramakrishna Math
Mylapore, Chennai-4

IX-3M 3C-6-2006
ISBN 81-7120-726-X

Printed in India at
Sri Ramakrishna Math Printing Press
Mylapore, Chennai-4

Publisher's Note

Our journal *Vedanta Kesari* is now in the 83rd year of its publication. For last several years, this monthly journal has been offering a bumper issue every December, spotlighting some theme related to philosophy, spirituality or culture. These issues have become immensely popular and, for larger circulation, have been issued later on in a book form.

The overwhelmingly enthusiastic welcome, both from Indian and foreign readers, that the December 1995 issue on 'Values' received was beyond our expectation. Such was the demand that whatever extra copies we had printed disappeared within three weeks of the journal's release. So we had to hurry with the book version which is in your hands.

The popularity of the 'Values' edition of the *Vedanta Kesari* was not only because of its valuable contents but also because the subject itself is of immense contemporary relevance and value. If this book provides the reader with some clear insights into values and helps in developing a strong value system, we shall consider our efforts amply rewarded.

Madras, 20 February 1996
Sri Ramakrishna's birthday

Contents

Introduction

Values. A terrible business. You can at best stammer when you talk about them.

— Wittgenstein (1889–1951)
Austrian-born British philosopher

Sometimes it is good to stammer about important things if the only alternative to it is to shut up and forget about the whole business. And, let's face it, values *are* important business. Terrible? Maybe. But important nonetheless.

Without values community life would be a chaos and individual life meaningless. A 'value'-less life is a valueless life. And who wants a life that's not worth a dime? We all want our life to have *some* meaning, *some* direction, *some* self-evolved authority for guidance. Values give us all this, so it would be foolish to close our eyes to them. Let's open our eyes, therefore, and stammer for a while.

We at once understand the difficulty. 'Values' and 'value' have been given so many connotations by common people and by philosophers, theologians, psychologists, economists, and other specialists that it is easy to get confused and lose interest in the whole thing. No wonder some find the whole business 'terrible.' But this is true of many other basic concepts as well. If you need a for-instance, there are several: justice, freedom, truth, reason. The meanings of these terms are complex and variable. It is possible to define them from a particular standpoint, but a comprehensive definition acceptable to academicians and, at the same time, intelligible to an ordinary Joe may be a near-impossibility.

This is one reason why philosophers warn against the careless use of the term 'values'. A. Campbell Garnett, author of *The Moral Nature of Man* (New York, 1952), writes:

> The term ['values'] is almost hopelessly ambiguous and should be avoided except where the context makes its shade of meaning perfectly clear, or where vagueness is an advantage in covering a broad field, as when one speaks of 'the general theory of values.'

The exception Garnett allows, that a vague term is useful in covering a broad field, is applicable to the volume in your hands; but the ambiguity here is limited to the breadth of our immediate concern—the situation in the world today and the challenges of the postmodern era. How do we cope with these? What values emerge from the lessons we learn in the contemporary world? Can we share one another's values the way we can share our ideas? What do we stand to gain by knowing about the different values people have in various parts of the world? These are some of the questions this volume concerns itself with.

But first, let's try to have at least a nodding acquaintance with 'values.'[1] A simple—and most preliminary—way of understanding 'values' is to know how they are related to 'interests'.

Interests and Values Are Linked

We all have a great many interests such as biological survival, physical and mental comfort, economic sufficiency, self-expression, companionship, and understanding of the natural and social worlds. Pursuits of these interests gives life its meaning and direction. The *satisfactions* or *attainments* of these interests are values, such as health, security, freedom, friendship, and knowledge. Thus interests and values are inextricably linked, and whatever applies to one is often applicable to the other.

Interests differ from person to person, and give a person his or her individuality. I may be interested in astronomy, you in growing dahlias, he in gambling, she in shopping. Our interests determine our occupations, our hobbies, our characters. My interests—what I care about

1. What follows is just one of the many ways of understanding the concept of 'value.' Those who wish to explore the subject further may see the article and bibliography on 'Value and Valuation' by William K. Frankena, in Paul Edwards, ed., *The Encyclopedia of Philosophy* (New York: The Macmillan Co. and The Free Press, 1967), 8: 229–32. By Indian authors there are two good books: Radhakamal Mukerjee, *The Dimensions of Value: A Unified Theory* (London: George Allen & Unwin Ltd., 1964) and K. R. Srinivasa Iyengar, *Metaphysics of Value* (Mysore: University of Mysore).

(or what I don't care about)—are *me,* they make me what I am, they unify my personality.

But interests also, simultaneously, divide my life. They divide my occupation from my hobbies, my play from my work, my public life from my private. I may be a businessman during the day, that being my occupation. But in the evenings or on weekends I could be a poet or an enthusiastic gardener, and be devoted to interests other than economic. We all feel it is good to have different interests, because they give variety and fullness to life.

Interests not only divide, they also unite and integrate. They bring people together and produce integrated groups or communities. Moreover, interests—and so values—are at once individual and general, personal and social. The specific individual interest which one person has in studying astronomy may be his or her special way of pursuing an interest (in this case, the understanding of natural world) which another person may pursue in quite a different way.

The immediate motive of pursuing an interest could be almost anything. It may be economic, scientific, hygienic, social, or spiritual. Suppose I study astronomy because of my love of knowledge, my curiosity to *know* things. I then discover that the knowledge I've acquired can help me earn my livelihood if I decide to teach or to write books. Thus the intellectual value of knowledge gets integrated with the economic value of self-maintenance. I might also get a chance to meet other astronomy enthusiasts. Exchanging ideas with them I build another interest—and therefore another value—into my growing system, that of friendship. My relentless sky-scanning might make me intensely aware of the unending vastness of the universe and produce in me detachment from everything inside this speck of dust called the planet Earth—and this might draw me toward spirituality. In this way, any specific interest can begin anywhere and end everywhere to embrace all the values of complete human living.

Interests and values, thus, do not remain detached or private. They get integrated, shared, and generalized. One value serves and is served by another, and with them forms a system of values, a total life. Every particular value is always an instance of a general value. Although there are many different occupations, fields of enquiry, social relationships, customs, ways of thinking, they all express general interests and embody general values, such as security, freedom, health, and knowledge.

One important point. The word 'interest' is used here in an inclusive sense. It designates non-neutral attitudes—state of being *for* or *against*. Thus 'values' can be said to cover the whole range of the likable, indifferent, and dislikable.

Classification of Values

When the value is on the plus side, such as beauty or freedom or nonviolence, it can be called positive (desires) value, when on the negative side, such as ugliness or bondage or violence, it can be called negative (aversions) value. When something is indifferent, exciting no interest whatever, it can be called valueless. But, of course, what is valueless from one point of view could be positively or negatively valuable from another.

Positive and negative values could be interpreted in another way too. There may be something desirable and yet not in our interest; attainment of it leads to sorrow and unfulfilment, and thus it is a negative value. On the other hand, there may be something about which we couldn't care less but which is for our good; attaining it produces joy and fulfilment—so it is a positive value.

Classifying values into positive and negative categories is not the only way. There are others. Some of the classification schemes distinguish ultimate, ideal values from mundane, operational values. Some distinguish essential-needs values from luxury-desires values. Some distinguish state-of-attainment (absolute) values from dynamics-of-pursuit (instrumental) values. Some distinguish self-oriented values from group-oriented values.

And, of course, we are aware of the classification of values by their content or source: aesthetic, economic, political, moral, spiritual. It is important to remember this, because it is often wrongly assumed that all values are moral or ethical in nature. The call for values in society or in education is usually made or is heard as a moral appeal. This is not correct. Although values characteristically carry demands and press claims, they can do so in amoral ways. Intellectual values such as truth, clarity, consistency, and rigour are often morally neutral. We do not usually consider errors or inconsistencies as immoral, unless they are intentional and meant to deceive someone. The whole of life is oriented and structured by values, so a concern for values need not be restricted merely to the moral dimension of experience.

Why Moral Values Dominate

It is not difficult to understand why there is a tendency to reduce all values to moral ones. Moral values regulate human conduct at much deeper levels of our personality than most other values do. So moral values tend to take precedence over other values. Values in other spheres that fail to respect our basic uniqueness as human beings, our dignity and worth, find themselves in conflict with moral requirements. Compromise, for instance, is an independent political value upto the point that it violates the value of moral integrity.

A kind of watchdog-nature of moral values becomes apparent specially in the sphere of personal values. When we start developing a particular way of life, we encounter situations where our values conflict with one another. We are called upon to make choices. This involves grading our values and fixing our priorities. Though ours are unforced decisions, there is clearly a moral aspect to the choices we make. Which do we choose, for instance, as the controlling value—status or integrity, power or love, service or ambition, freedom or security, and so on. In itself there may be no moral issue involved in choosing to relax by taking a nap. But if that is all a person does, specially while being needed elsewhere, his or her choice of values enters the moral sphere.

How Values Are Identified

Is it easy to know what my values are? Not quite. Values are so close, so intimate, that it is easy to overlook them. They define the nature of our intention and action so subtly that they may disappear behind our everyday choices and tasks. Those who develop a shallow, mechanical, impulsive mode of living do not know what their values are and, moreover, they don't know that they do not know. Nor are they really bothered.

One way of becoming aware of our values is through a process of comparison and contrast. A child's identity takes form only when it defines itself as separate from its parents. In the same way, we become aware of the specific qualities that our way of life possesses when we contrast it with others'. We then learn to self-question. What is so important to me that it could never be sacrificed for something else? Anything? What seems to count more as I review events—order or freedom, the immediate or the ultimate, my interest or others' interest? How do I approach social problems—with a pragmatic spirit or with an idealistic one?

Answers to such questions can be found when we examine our thoughts, actions, and feelings, for it is through these that our values are expressed. Richard Morrill explains:

> Although values are not themselves beliefs or judgments, they necessarily come to expression in and through thought. Although values are not feelings or emotions, they inevitably involve desires and fears. Although values cannot be defined as deeds, they always are mediated through specific acts. To paraphrase and expand on Kant: Values without reason would be blind, without feeling would be impotent, and without deeds would be empty.[2]

---

2. Richard L. Morrill, *Teaching Values in College* (San Francisco: Jossey-Bass Publishers, 1980), 72–73.

Values exist as demands, because they have around them an aura of ought-ness in the choice among alternatives. Values provide an in-built standard of reference and judgment for our actions. Thus they are integrally tied to choice and action, and to our constant process of self-appraisal. I cannot be said to fully hold a value unless my actions are influenced by it, and I can take no meaningful action except in the name of some value.

Our beliefs and attitudes can easily be suspended, rationalized or contradicted in action and ignored in self-evaluation. But not so our values, because my values are *me*. As I discover my values I discover my total human identity. I really get to know myself: where I stand, what I count for, and what counts for me. My values determine the way I'm able to put my life together. They regulate my choices and actions, and they are the standards against which I can measure my actions. I am able to pose basic questions about my purposes and loyalties, my sources of worth and self-respect.

But values are by no means static, permanent, unchangeable. We may have good reasons for abandoning a value or incorporating a new one in our system, but that process involves its own justification and careful reckoning. Of course, unlike our beliefs and attitudes, values are not chosen or abandoned casually, because something very vital is at stake here—the self's own estimate of itself.

From what is said so far, it might appear that my values are solely concerned with me, they are my own private something. Not so. I am not an island. I live in the world. My values *connect* me to the world around, they connect everyone to everyone else. There's a huge network of 'value'-bridges out there. Through values the world becomes meaningful and relevant. Without them the world would be a formless chaos, a place where any action would be possible at any time and all actions would be arbitrary.

The world offers innumerable possibilities both for satisfaction and frustration, creation and destruction, life and death. Values link my needs and purposes with the opportunities and obstacles of the world. They also link me to other people. Through common allegiance to values, an 'I' and a 'you' can become a 'we', and jointly share tasks and demands, joys and sorrows.

Value Systems and Social Change

We have seen that interests and values are interlinked. Now the question is, how free am I in developing my existing interests and cultivating new ones? Well, not as free as I would like to be. The simple truth is that the society in which I live plays a great role in shaping my interests and, consequently, influencing my value system.

Societies in different parts of the world have acquired distinct identities, because each society thrives in a different mileau with its own historical and cultural baggage. Since it is customary—and also a bit old-timey—to make much about the differences between the East and the West (in spite of sharp differences *within* the East and *within* the West), we hear terms such as Eastern values and Western values.

But this trend is now on the way out, thanks to technology, which has provided us with easy means of communication and quick, comfortable travel from anywhere to anywhere on this planet. The dividing lines between cultures and societies are getting blurred.[3] A global culture and a global society may not have arrived so far, and perhaps never will, but a phenomenal increase in international trade, tourism and satellite TV networks has ensured sufficient intermingling of cultures and social identities.

As a result, new interests are being created, and old interests are being abandoned or their usefulness questioned. Western values are invading Eastern societies and vice versa. Where this amalgamation process will take us all, time alone can say. What is in my hands is to take charge of my own life and to ensure that the current changes do not shunt my life-wagon on to an undesirable track. I don't have to insulate myself from the world around. All I need to do is to sift healthy, nourishing values from unhealthy, debilitating ones and integrate them into my value system.[4] So instead of being a hindrance, multiculturalism might prove to be a blessing, after all. Taking proper care of our own life and choosing the right values to guide it—this is something every one of us has the capacity to do.

A good way to begin is to learn from the experiences of people engaged in different fields in different parts of the world. What are their views, perceptions, insights

---

3. It is the fear of losing one's identity in a global mix of cultures that has provoked, as a reaction, a resurgence of militant nationalism, religious fundamentalism, and aggressive racism in many parts of the world.
4. This is not easy. What is healthy and nourishing may not always be attractive and welcoming on the surface; what is unhealthy and debilitating, on the other hand, might well be alluring and deceptively harmless. Sufficient maturity is essential to make the right choices.

concerning values in the fields they are actively associated with? What values sustain them in the midst of the global changes occurring all around? It is possible—indeed, it is certain—that many of the lessons emerging from their experiences will be relevant to our own life-situations. Assimilating those lessons will enrich our lives and help us create a more wholesome value system capable of withstanding new pressures, facing new challenges, and making every one of us a better person.

This Volume

That is what prompted us to invite articles dealing with values in different fields of human endeavour. Not all fields are represented here, of course, but a good many are. Fifteen, to be exact: Administration, Business, Cinema, Education, Family, Industry, Journalism, Law, Law Enforcement, Literature, Medicine, Music, Science and Technology, Society, and Sport. We are grateful to the contributors for readily responding to our invitation to share their ideas.

But before we go on to study the role of values in different fields, we must get a clear idea of what 'values' are and how they are related to Reality and social norms. That is the subject of the thought-provoking article on the facing page.

1

Values, Yoga and Reality

SWAMI BHAJANANANDA

Two recent events have shocked human conscience all over the world for their utter senselessness and potential danger to humanity. One is the poison gas attack on commuters in the subway system of Tokyo in March 1995 that killed a dozen people and injured more than five thousand people. The other event is the bomb blast that shattered a federal building in Oklahoma in the United States killing more than 130 people including many children in April 1995.

The poison gas attack was the work of a Japanese religious sect consisting mostly of young people. The surprising thing about this sect is that it could attract some of the most brilliant, highly educated young men to its ranks.

Social scientists trying to investigate what went wrong with these smart and talented youths put the blame on the present educational system in Japan. Although rated as one of the best in the world, the Japanese educational system lacked proper value orientation, they pointed out. A *New York Times* report quoted a long-time professor of philosophy at Sophia University in Tokyo as saying, 'It reflects a profound crisis in the educational system. Many Japanese students are absorbing even greater amounts of information, but they don't acquire the ability to make value judgments on basic human values, like responsibility for human life or respect for freedom of the individual.'

Far more foreboding is the Oklahoma bombing. It is said to have been engineered by a fanatical paramilitary group whose members have been described by the New York City Police Commissioner as, 'basically white supremacists, Christian fundamentalists, some of them totally hostile to the federal government... They have been a kind of low-level infection, as it were, on the body politic.' The emergence of this national network of fanatical militia men adds a new threat to civic order in a society already plagued by the collapse of family life, racism, drug addiction, juvenile gang wars, crime and violence. Reviewing the present situation in American society, Allan Bloom, author of the well-known book *The Closing of the American Mind,* says that the 'most important and most astonishing phenomenon of our time, all the more astounding in being unnoticed, is that there is now an entirely new language of good and evil, originating in an attempt to get *beyond good and evil* and preventing us from talking with any conviction about good and evil any more... The new language is that of value relativism, and it constitutes a change in our view of things moral and political as great as the one that took place when Christianity replaced Greek and Roman paganism.'

More than the increase in immorality, it is the elimination of the notion of guilt from modern man's mind that Allan Bloom finds profoundly disturbing. A drastic change in modern man's concept of morality is now taking place. A form of behaviour or life-style which had till now been regarded as an aberration or perversion is now accepted as normal and moral. For instance, thousands of men and women in Western countries cohabit without the compulsion of marriage and without any compunction. According to Barbara Dafoe Whitehead of the Institute for American Values, there has been a 'shift in the social metric.' At some point in the 1970s Americans changed their minds about such disruptive behaviour as divorce and unwed motherhood. 'What had once been regarded as hostile to children's best interests was now considered as essential to adults' happiness,' says Ms. Whitehead.

About this shift in social metric an eminent conservative leftist Christopher Lasch says in his posthumous publication *The Revolt of the Elites and the Betrayal of Democracy,* 'A lust for immediate gratification pervades American society from top to bottom. There is a universal concern with the self—with self-fulfilment and, more recently, with self-esteem, slogans of a society incapable of generating a sense of civic obligation.'

More than a century ago Nietzsche spoke of the need for 'transvaluation of all values.' Perhaps a kind of transvaluation is going on all over the world. At any rate, we need to have a fresh look at the value system that governs modern society. Every culture is in a state of equilibrium between its system of values and its system of beliefs. Science and technology have considerably altered modern man's views on Life and the universe. This has resulted in drastic changes in the system of beliefs, but the value system has not responded adequately to these changes. This is the root cause of the 'crisis in values' we see in all departments of modern life. We do not propose to undertake a comprehensive study of this crisis. Our purpose here is only to offer some conceptual clarification regarding values and their relation to views on Reality and social norms.

Meaning of the Term 'Value'

There is a good deal of vagueness and confusion about the word 'values'. The well-known American psychologist Abraham Maslow writes: 'However, "values" are defined in many ways, and mean different things to different people. As a matter of fact, it is so confusing semantically that I am convinced we will soon give up this catch-all word in favour of more precise and more operational definitions for each of the many submeanings that have been attached to it.'[1]

'Values' is most commonly used as a substitute for the words 'virtues' and 'morality'. The latter are plainer words, and yet many people, especially politicians, seldom use them—either because of the credibility gap or because of the religious overtones of these words. So, instead of these plain words, they use the word 'values'.

But values do not mean only virtues. One way to understand what 'value' means is to distinguish values from facts. When we say that the Gita was composed before the 3rd century B.C. or that Taj Mahal was built by Shah Jahan, we are making a factual statement. But when we say that it was wrong on the part of Arjuna to lay down arms or that Taj Mahal is the most beautiful building in the world, we are making a value judgment. In fact, we live in two worlds: the world of facts and the world of values. These two worlds do not always correspond to each other. Values often lead us beyond the world of facts and point to goals beyond the senses. Another way to understand what 'value' means is to trace its origin. The term 'value' entered philosophical thinking by way of economics. In economics it is used to mean (a) the capacity of an object to satisfy a human need or desire (this is known as value in use), or (b) money (value in exchange). It is the first meaning that is relevant here.

It is well known that man has a hierarchy of needs which provide the motivation for his behaviour. According to Abraham Maslow, these needs, in the ascending order, are: biological needs, security, love, esteem, knowledge, aesthetic needs, self-actualization and transcendence.[2] Of these the lower needs connected with man's physical existence, such as the need for food, clothing, shelter, etc. are called 'basic needs' or simply 'needs'. The needs higher to these constitute *values.*

However, values are not mere higher 'needs' or desires. Rather, they imply what is *desirable* or *valuable.* Being desired is only a part of the meaning of valuable. Not all things that are desired are valuable, and some things that are not desired by many people today are undoubtedly valuable.

In the words of sociologist Clyde Kluckhon,

> Values do not consist in desires but rather in the *desirable,* that is, what we not only want but feel that it is right and proper to want for ourselves and for others... [Values are] abstract standards that transcend the impulses of the moment and ephemeral situations.[3]

It is the sense of 'ought' that distinguishes values from ordinary desires or needs. For instance, truth is something not only desirable but we feel that we ought to be truthful. Values are inner imperatives which urge us to seek higher goals. The distinguished Indian social scientist Radhakamal Mukerjee offers the following clarification:

> The psychological and social sciences dealing with values define them as mere preferences, as desirable goals, emotions and interests. The humanistic disciplines, on the other hand, define them as functioning imperatives or 'oughts.'[4]

We have seen that values are higher needs and are also inner imperatives or oughts. They have one more characteristic: they belong to the whole society or community or even the whole humanity. It is not what any individual thinks as desirable that is called value, but what the whole community or majority of people think as desirable. That is to say, values are certain social norms or standards. Values belong to culture. Explaining this, the authors of a popular book on sociology state: 'A cultural value may be defined as a widely held belief or sentiment that some activities, relationships, feelings or goals are important to the community's identity or well-being.'[5]

Combining all the three characteristics of values, we may now give a comprehensive definition: Values are the higher normative needs of humanity which individuals experience as inner moral or aesthetic imperatives or goal seeking.

Another concept frequently confused with values is the 'ideal'. An ideal is nothing but a *value chosen as the goal* of life by an individual.

Values as Expressions of the Evolutionary Urge

According to some thinkers values, as expressions of the inborn desire in man for self-improvement, the inherent urge to seek higher and higher levels of fulfilment, represent life's higher evolutionary urge. Says the eminent biologist Julian Huxley: 'We find values not only emerging from the evolutionary process but playing an active part in its latest phase; we know as an immediate and obvious fact that there are higher and lower values, we discover as a result of scientific analysis that there are more or less desirable and valuable directions in evolution.'[6]

Radhakamal Mukerjee adds: 'Such a directive quality of adjustment of organism to the environment at the dimension of human social evolution is called *values* which influence the course of evolution towards greater individuality and openness of self and purposive direction of self and environment... Rudiments of values are discernible among the brainy animals. But no animal, including the lower primates, can develop a set of values that direct and regulate behaviour around long-term goals or evolve a symbolic complex helping them to accumulate, reorganize and anticipate experiences.'[7]

That is to say, values are not mere individual desires and fancies but are expressions of the creative power of universal Life. The river of life is flowing through all, and values mark the higher points of its rising tide. There is in man an intrinsic urge to seek higher levels of existence, higher levels of consciousness and higher levels of happiness. Values are manifestations of this urge.

It may, however, be mentioned here that this lofty view of values is no longer in vogue now. The tendency in recent years is to treat values merely as interests or desires. R. B. Perry, who is one of the proponents of this view, says: 'A thing—anything—has value or is valuable when it is the object of an interest, any interest. Or whatever is an object of interest is ipso facto valuable.'[8] Here interest includes both likes and dislikes.

Types of Values

Values do not belong to one field of experience alone but to different fields. Hence we have several kinds of values. The most well-known of these are moral values, known as virtues, such as truthfulness, kindness, equality, etc. Apart from these, there are social values, aesthetic values, cognitive values, and spiritual values. Each class of values pertains to a particular dimension of personality. The pursuit of all the five classes of values mentioned above is necessary for the all-round development of personality.

Not all values, however, are of equal importance. Some of the values are regarded as an end in themselves; these are called absolute values. Values which are regarded as a means for the attainment of some higher goal are called instrumental values. Which values are regarded as absolute and which as instrumental depends upon the culture to which the values belong.

The Greek culture from very ancient times regarded Truth, Goodness and Beauty as absolute values. From the Greeks this concept passed on to the Romans and to later Western culture. Christian religion posited love of God as the absolute value and love for man as an instrumental value. These ideas also passed on to Western culture, but they never became its dominant characteristics.

Indian culture has adopted, right from very ancient times, a two-tier system of values which are known as *puruṣārthas*. The lower tier consists of three values: *kāma* (sensuous pleasure), *artha* (wealth) and *dharma* (morality). Hindu scriptures clearly state that *kāma* and *artha* should be governed by *dharma*. This triad (*trivarga*) of values is meant for ordinary people. For those who have developed dispassion for the world, Hindu culture offers the upper tier which forms the highest value (*parama puruṣārtha*), namely, *mukti* or *mokṣa,* everlasting freedom. There is hardly anyone who does not want to be free from sorrow. *Mukti*, however, is not freedom from ordinary sorrow but from the very possibility of being reborn on earth. *Mukti* is an absolute value. The lower three values may be regarded as instrumental values, although they do not necessarily lead to *mukti*.

Values and Reality

Though there are similarities between the Indian and Western approaches to value, we have to keep in mind that the whole concept of value is characteristically Western. Plato is believed to have originated the study of values, but it was only towards the end of the 19th century that it was reorganized as an independent discipline under the name Axiology. Since then several Western philosophers have regarded values as the main object of philosophical enquiry and as the ultimate goal of life. But are values an end in themselves? Can mere pursuit of values be regarded as the ultimate goal of life? Are not values only pointers to an ultimate thing valued?

The last question may be answered first. In the ordinary practical world we find that the word 'value' usually refers to something which is valued. For instance, when the shopkeeper tells us that the price of a kilo of potatoes is five rupees, what he means is that potato is a valuable thing. The five rupees we pay is only a symbol of the abstract idea of its value. The potato is the real thing; it satisfies our hunger. The money we pay, its value, is only a token; it cannot by itself satisfy our hunger.

This is true of higher values also. Values are intangible abstract concepts which have their ultimate source in certain aspect of Reality. Values have no existence apart from the Reality they represent. Values only stimulate the quest for lasting fulfilment, but they cannot by themselves give that fulfilment. They only tantalize like a mirage, and goad people to something beyond them. But lasting fulfilment can come only through the transcendental realization of the ultimate Reality.

This insight into the ultimate meaning and purpose of life has always provided Indian culture its main thrust. From very ancient times orientation to the ultimate Reality has provided the basic discipline to the best minds in India. It was assumed that if Reality orientation was done in the proper way, value orientation would follow in a natural way. Orientation to Reality had always formed the core subject of the Indian system of education until the beginning of the modern age. And, as the stories of children in the Upaniṣads indicate, this orientation to Reality began early in boyhood. In the *Chāndogya Upaniṣad* we find a boy named Satyakāma gains direct knowledge of Brahman through communion with nature, and another boy, Upakosala, feels depressed because of his teacher's refusal to instruct him about Brahman.

By contrast, value orientation has been the dominant characteristic of Western culture. It is doubtful whether the ancient Greeks attained direct realization of the ultimate Reality. As discussions in Plato's works indicate, Greek culture was primarily value-oriented, and this tradition became a heritage for Western people. Although Christianity produced many illumined saints, direct mystical experience of the ultimate Reality never became an essential aspect of Western culture.

Right from Plato's time Western culture has cherished Beauty, Truth and Goodness as the ultimate values. Art, science and social service are regarded as the pursuit of these three values respectively. In all these three fields the West has many achievements to its credit. But it has not found the way to lasting fulfilment and peace, nor has it been able to stem the tide of degradation. A few years ago the Foundation for Advanced Information and Research, Japan, published a series of reports based on research conducted by several Study Groups. One of the reports states: 'The affluent society has altered the desires, behavioural patterns and social structures of its people. These changes include the formation of a new upper class, the fragmentation of values, and the appearance of a pathological social phenomenon, the so-called "advanced nation's syndrome," in rich societies... This malaise affects not only the economies of the countries involved, but its symptoms penetrate the political and social spheres as well. As a result, the advanced industrial societies are faced not only with declining economic vitality, but also with a variety of manifestations of anomie, such as decreasing political unity, terrorism, crime, juvenile delinquency, suicide, anxiety and depression, alcoholism, drug addiction, the loss of the will to work, and sexual confusion.'

Science and technology have orientated the minds of people in the West almost wholly to the physical world, and Western culture has become thoroughly materialistic. In such a situation traditional values have become inoperative resulting in a crisis of values. The basic cause of this crisis is that the Western conception of values is not rooted in a clear perception or understanding of the ultimate Reality.

Here comes the importance of the Vedantic vision of Brahman, the ultimate Reality, as *Sat-cit-ānanda* (Being-Awareness-Bliss Absolute). This view can provide the reality support that the Western concept of Beauty, Truth and Goodness as ultimate values very much stands in need of. Beauty, Truth and Goodness may be regarded as *Sat, Cit* and *Ānanda* perceived through the veil of Māyā. Vedantic scriptures state that Brahman manifests itself in the empirical world as *asti, bhāti,* and *priyam.*[9] These may be said to correspond to Beauty, Truth and Goodness.

Yoga, the Connecting Link Between Values and Reality

The main thesis we have been trying to establish is this: Value orientation must be supported by Reality orientation. Values have no value in themselves. It is the Reality behind the values that gives them power. Values must be rooted in Reality.

This principle applies not only at the higher level of philosophical thinking where Beauty, Truth and Goodness appear as abstract concepts or ideals, but also at the lower level of practising the simple virtues of ordinary life. It is not enough to preach to young people about values or virtues; they should be shown how to make the values or virtues real in their lives. It is no use telling a young man, 'Be fearless,' unless the deep-rooted cause of fear in him is removed. What is the use of talking to a person about the 'value' of love if he has received no love from his parents or other people?

In this context it is worth quoting what Swami Vivekananda said in one of his lectures on Rāja Yoga:

> We hear 'Be good,' and 'Be good,' and 'Be good,' taught all over the world. There is hardly a child, born in any country in the world, who has not been told, 'Do not steal,' 'Do not tell a lie,' but nobody tells the child how he can help doing them. Talking will not help him... Only when we teach him to control his mind do we really help him.[10]

In order to attain value fulfilment we have to confront the reality that it represents. This calls for self-discipline in the form of self-control, self-knowledge and inward concentration. This kind of self-discipline in due course brings about transformation of one's consciousness which is what Yoga means. On this point Swami Vivekananda says,

> We have to get the power to become moral; until we do that, we cannot control our actions. Yoga alone enables us to carry into practice the teachings of morality. To become moral is the object of Yoga.[11]

Yoga is, thus, the connecting link between values and Reality. Yoga transforms value experience into mystic experience. Yoga give us the power to go beyond values and realize the Reality which they symbolize. Without Yoga values remain mere dreams of poets and preachers.

Unfortunately, there is much misunderstanding about Yoga in the East as well as in the West. For many people Yoga means nothing more than some postural exercises. But true Yoga is an inner discipline for the transformation of consciousness through self-knowledge, self-control and self-directed activity. Though there are special techniques for this transformation such as Jñāna Yoga, Bhakti Yoga, Rāja Yoga, etc., any work, any activity, can be done as Yoga. Education—both teaching and learning—can be done as Yoga. Pursuit of art can be done as Yoga. Pursuit of science can be done as Yoga. Social service can be done as Yoga. Indeed, one's whole life can be converted into Yoga. In the *Gītā,* Kṛṣṇa describes the whole creation as 'Divine Yoga.'[12] Of course, the 'Yoga' that is spoken of here is only of the preliminary type. But it is nevertheless important. Its importance lies in the fact that it gives to the soul proper Reality orientation.

The Two-level Unfoldment

The transformation of consciousness that Yoga brings about is, from the standpoint of Advaita Vedanta, a form of unveiling or unfolding of the inner Self. According to

Vedanta, man's real nature is neither the body nor the mind but the Self known as the Ātman. This true Self is of the nature of pure, unchanging, self-luminous awareness which is immortal and is the source of all knowledge, all happiness, all power. Furthermore, all individual selves are only reflections of one universal Supreme Self. However, owing to beginningless ignorance known as Māyā or *avidyā,* the inner Self remains veiled. Cognition removes a bit of this ignorance; then the Self manifests itself and its light reveals the object as knowledge. This is how every kind of knowledge takes place. Explaining this process, Swami Vivekananda says,

> Knowledge is inherent in man; no knowledge comes from outside; it is all inside. What we say a man 'knows', should in strict psychological parlance be what he 'discovers', by taking the cover off his own soul, which is a mine of infinite knowledge.[13]

In other words, every kind of knowledge—even the lowest form of sense experience—is the result of the self-manifestation of the Ātman.

What, then, is the difference between ordinary empirical knowledge and higher transcendental knowledge? The answer is, although the manifestation of the Ātman takes place in both the types of experience, the nature of knowledge is determined by the type of ignorance involved. According to Vedanta, ignorance is of two kinds: empirical ignorance (known as *tūlāvidyā*) and causal ignorance (known as *mūlāvidyā*). The first one is ignorance regarding empirical objects, whereas the second one is ignorance concerning the ultimate Reality, the true nature of the Ātman.

In empirical knowledge the removal of only *tūlāvidyā,* empirical ignorance, takes place. This is the fundamental

mental process taking place in education. Learning removes only empirical ignorance, but this is enough to give us knowledge of the external world and bring out the talents and capacities inherent in individual minds. This was, perhaps, what Swami Vivekananda meant when he gave the famous definition, 'Education is the manifestation of the *perfection* already in man.'

But this kind of empirical knowledge which we gain through education does not remove causal ignorance. Only transcendental knowledge gained through Yoga can remove causal ignorance. When causal ignorance is removed, the Ātman reveals or manifests itself in all its glory. This experience known as Self-realization or God-realization is the essential meaning and purpose of Religion. The idea that 'Religion is [transcendental] realization' has gained popularity in modern times mainly through the teachings of Sri Ramakrishna and Swami Vivekananda. Swamiji did not, however, want religious experience to be restricted to the transcendental plane alone. He wanted that the higher knowledge should manifest itself through the attitudes and actions of the individual in the world, and should help him to face the problem of social life. Hence Swamiji gave a new definition of religion: 'Religion is the manifestation of the Divinity already in man.' Explaining this, he stated in another context:

> My ideal, indeed, can be put into a few words, and that is: to preach unto mankind their divinity, and how to make it manifest in every movement of life.[14]

So then, according to Swami Vivekananda, education and religion are two phases of a single process of Self-revelation or Self-realization. Pursuit of values and quest for the ultimate Reality are both manifestations of man's innate evolutionary urge at two planes of existence. Such a view transforms education into a spiritual discipline, removes the distinction between the secular and the sacred, and makes one's life a ceaseless striving for higher degrees of love, knowledge and happiness. Such a holistic view alone can make life meaningful, harmonious and peaceful. This is the integral philosophy of life that the world is very much in need of now.

The Ethos of a People

In this context certain pertinent questions arise. If India is so culturally rich, how come she is materially so poor? If India has the credit of developing the high philosophy of divinity of the soul and oneness of life, how is it that some of the worst forms of social injustice, exploitation and discrimination have persisted in Indian society for centuries? How is it that a nation with the highfalutin motto 'Truth alone triumphs' has now come to be rated as one of the most corrupt and dishonest in the world? Even from ancient times in India nonviolence and contemplation have coexisted with incessant wars and thuggery and, now, terrorism and extremism. This paradox, and the paradox of a nation which taught harmony of religions to the world being perpetually rocked by religious unrest and communal riots, need an explanation.

The explanation lies in the peculiar ethos of the Indian people, which has not been studied properly. However, before proceeding further, we have to understand what 'ethos of a people' really means. The phrase was introduced perhaps by the German philosopher Hegel who spoke of every child being 'suckled at the breast of the universal Ethos.' According to Hegel, 'The wisest men of antiquity have given judgment that wisdom and virtue consist in living agreeably to the Ethos of one's people.'[15]

The original German word used was *sitten* which means moral habitudes of thought and action. There is no English word that fully expresses this idea and, instead of having recourse to the German, it has become customary to use a Greek term *ethos.*

The word 'ethos' has been defined in Webster's dictionary as, 'the distinguishing character, sentiment, moral nature or guiding beliefs of a person or group or institution.' More simply stated, it means the moral temper of a race, or nation, or community. It represents the sum total of the moral attitudes of a group, the way they react to various problems and situations in life. Mackenzie says that the ethos of a people 'constitutes the atmosphere in which the best members of a race habitually live... it constitutes the universe of their moral activities.'[16]

India has an ancient culture rich in spiritual wealth unmatched by any other culture in the world. And its value system which is based on, and aims at, direct realization of the ultimate Reality, holds great promise for the future welfare of humanity. However, we can't talk in the same vein about the ethos of the Indian people. For there are grave defects and drawbacks in the Indian ethos.

The Indian ethos favours the cultivation of certain values such as renunciation, charity, chastity, filial duties, and spiritual disciplines. People in this country can be more easily prompted to pursue these values. But the ethos has not been so favourable to the pursuit of some other values such as justice, equality, scientific objectivity, dignity of labour, and collective responsibility. The inadequacy of the ethos of this land is the main cause of this nation's loss of political power, loss of economic prosperity, loss of intellectual vigour and moral stamina, and dismal performance in international sports and games. Social tyranny, caste war, exploitation of the poor, bride burning, and corruption at all levels of administration still persist in modern India mainly because of the supportive nature of the ethos of the people.

Several factors have contributed to the creation of the Indian ethos the most significant of which are: the strange institution of caste which prevented vertical social mobility, the evils of priestcraft, the segregation of people caused by racial, linguistic and regional differences, prolonged submission to alien rulers, and the popularization of a philosophy of illusion among the masses. Whatever be the contributory factors, it is necessary to know the limitations of the ethos which have been the main cause of the nation's failures in several fields.

If India is to attain economic prosperity, social well-being, intellectual advancement, national integration, and the rejuvenation of her ancient spiritual culture and values, drastic changes in the ethos of the people must be brought about. This was one of the major tasks Swami Vivekananda took upon himself. Swamiji himself pointed out that the reformers who had preceded him had made 'the serious mistake of holding religion accountable for all the horrors of priestcraft and degeneration' and tried to pull down the indestructible edifice of religion. The same mistake had been committed by the German sociologist Max Weber a few years before Swamiji expressed his ideas. In his book *The Religion of India* Weber raised the question why India, in spite of having an advanced culture and wealth, failed to develop a technological civilization, and he held the Hindu religion responsible for the failure. Swami Vivekananda, however, showed that religion was not at fault. The degradation of India took place not because of religion but because the life-giving spiritual principles of religion had not been properly applied in practical life.[17] Swamiji saw that India's spiritual culture was the repository of eternal values which could help to rejuvenate not only India but the whole world. This does not, however, mean Swamiji believed that everything was all right with India. The word 'ethos' had not become popular during his time but he never overlooked the fact that the individual temperament and social attitudes of the people of India were defective in several respects, and he never hesitated to apply the corrective wherever necessary.

Modern India is a bundle of contradictions. But if we keep in mind the distinction between values and the ethos of the people, it becomes possible for us to see the contradictions in the right perspective.

References

1. Abraham Maslow, *The Farther Reaches of Human Nature* (New York: Penguin Books, 1982), 106.
2. Abraham Maslow, *Motivation and Personality* (New York: Harper and Row, 1970).
3. Clyde Kluckhon, *Culture and Behaviour* (New York: The Free Press of Glenco, 1962), 289.

4. Radhakamal Mukerjee, *The Dimensions of Value* (London: George Allen and Unwin, 1964).
5. Leonard Broom and Philip Selznic, *Principles of Sociology* (New York: Harper and Row, 1970), 54.
6. Julian Huxley, *Evolution and Ethics* (New York: Macmillan, 1947), 32.
7. Radhakamal Mukerjee, op. cit.
8. Ralph Barton Perry, *The Realms of Value* (New York: Greenwood Press, 1968).
9. Cf. *Dṛg-Dṛśya-Viveka,* 20.
10. *Complete Works of Swami Vivekananda,* 8 vols. (Calcutta: Advaita Ashrama, 1973), 1: 171 (hereafter cited as CW).
11. CW, 8: 43.
12. Paśya me yogam-aiśvaram, *Gita,* 9: 5; 11: 8.
13. CW, 1: 28.
14. CW, 7: 498.
15. Quoted in J. A. Mackenzie, *A Manual of Ethics* (Delhi: Oxford University Press, 1973), 330.
16. Ibid.
17. CW, 5: 22, 14, 47.

2

Values for a Nonviolent Society

TENZIN GYATSO

His Holiness The Dalai Lama

My ideas about universal responsibility have evolved from the ancient traditions of India. As a Buddhist monk my entire training has its roots in the culture of this great country. Emotionally too I feel very close to this country. In ancient times India produced many great thinkers, whose insights contributed much to humanity's spiritual evolution. Even today, India is an inspiration, for in the face of great odds, democracy thrives.

Ahimsa or nonviolence is a powerful idea that Mahatma Gandhi made familiar throughout the world. Nonviolence does not mean the mere absence of violence. It is something more positive, more meaningful than that.

The true expression of nonviolence is compassion. Some people seem to think that compassion is just a passive emotional response instead of a rational stimulus to action. To experience genuine compassion is to develop a feeling of closeness to others combined with a sense of responsibility for their welfare. True compassion develops when we accept that other people are just like ourselves in wanting happiness and not wanting suffering and that they have every right to pursue these.

Compassion compels us to reach out to all living beings, including our so-called enemies, those people who upset or hurt us. Irrespective of what they do to you, if you remember that all beings like you are only trying to be happy, you will find it much easier to develop compassion towards them. Usually our sense of compassion is limited and biased. We extend such feelings only towards our family and friends or those who are helpful to us. People we perceive as enemies and others to whom we are indifferent are excluded from our concern. That is not genuine compassion. True compassion is universal in scope. It is accompanied by a feeling of responsibility. To act altruistically, concerned only for the welfare of others, with no selfish or ulterior motive, is to affirm a sense of universal responsibility.

I am a Buddhist monk, so cultivation of compassion is an important part of my daily practice. One aspect involves merely sitting quietly in my room, meditating. That can be very good and very comfortable, but the true aim of cultivating compassion is to develop the courage to think of others and to do something for them. For example, as the Dalai Lama I have a responsibility to my people, some of whom are living as refugees and some of whom have remained in Tibet under Chinese occupation. This responsibility means that I have to confront and deal with many problems.

Certainly, it is easier to meditate than to actually do something for others. Sometimes I feel that to merely meditate on compassion is to take the passive option. Our meditation should form the basis for action, for seizing the opportunity to do something. The meditator's motivation, his sense of universal responsibility, should be expressed in deeds.

Whether we are rich or poor, educated or uneducated, whatever our nationality, colour, social status or ideology may be, the purpose of our lives is to be happy. For this, material development plays an important role. But at the same time it is more important to cultivate a corresponding inner development. Unless our minds are stable and calm, no matter how comfortable our physical conditions may be, they will give us no pleasure. Therefore, the key to a happy life, now and in the future, is to develop a happy mind.

One of the most powerful emotions disturbing our mental tranquillity is hatred. The antidote is compassion. We should not think of compassion as being only the preserve of the sacred and religious. It is one of our basic human qualities. Human nature is essentially loving and gentle. Despite the apparent prevalence of anger and hatred in the world, I do not agree with people who assert that human beings are innately aggressive. From the moment of our birth we require love and affection. This is true of us all, right up to the day we die. Without love we could not survive. Human beings are social creatures and concern for each other is the very basis of our life together. If we stop to think, compared to the numerous acts of kindness on which we depend and which we take so much for granted, acts of hostility are relatively few. To see the truth of this we only need to observe the love and affection parents shower on their children and the many other acts of loving and caring that we take for granted.

I am sure everybody agrees that we need to overcome violence, but if we are to eliminate it completely, we should first analyze whether or not it has any value. From a strictly practical perspective, we find that on occasions violence indeed appears useful. One can solve a problem quickly with force. At the same time, however, such success is often at the expense of the rights and welfare of others. As a result, even though one problem has been solved, the seed of another has been planted.

On the other hand, if one's cause is supported by sound reasoning, there is no point in using violence. People who rely on force are those who have no motive other than selfish desire and who cannot achieve their goal through logical reasoning. Even when family and friends disagree, those with valid reasons can cite them one after the other and argue their case point by point, whereas those with little rational support soon fall prey to anger. Thus anger is not a sign of strength but of weakness.

Ultimately, it is important to examinc one's own motivation and that of one's opponent. There are many kinds of violence and nonviolence, but one cannot distinguish them from external factors alone. If one's motivation is negative, the action it produces is, in the deepest sense, violent, even though it may appear to be smooth and gentle. Conversely, if one's motivation is sincere and positive but the circumstances require harsh behaviour, essentially one is practising nonviolence. No matter what the case may be, I feel that a compassionate concern for the benefit of others—not simply for oneself—is the sole justification for the use of force.

So far I have mentioned how a positive outlook can affect an individual. It is also true that the more compassionate a society, the happier its members will be. The development of human society is based entirely on people helping each other. Every individual has a responsibility to help guide the community in the right direction and we must each assume that responsibility. If we lose this essential humanity that is our foundation, society as a whole will collapse.

What point will there then be in pursuing material improvement and from whom can we demand our rights? Action motivated by compassion and responsibility will ultimately bring good results. Anger and jealousy may be effective in the short term, but will ultimately bring us only trouble.

Fear is another major obstacle to our inner development. And fear arises when we view everyone else with suspicion. It is compassion that creates the sense of trust that allows us to open up to others and reveal our problems, doubts and uncertainties. Without it we cannot communicate with each other honestly and openly. Therefore, developing compassion is one of the most effective ways of reducing fear.

Compassion is a fundamentally human quality, so its development is not restricted to those who practise religion.

Nevertheless, religious traditions have a special role to play in encouraging its development. The common factor among all religions is that, whatever the philosophical differences between them, they are primarily concerned with helping their followers become better human beings. Consequently, all religions encourage the practice of kindness, generosity and concern for others. This is why I find conflicts based on religious differences to be so sad and futile.

It is my belief, for the world in general, that compassion is more important than 'religion'. The population of our planet is over five billion. Of these perhaps one billion actively and sincerely follow a formal religion. The remaining over four billion are not believers in the true sense. If we regard the development of compassion and other good qualities as the business only of religion, these over four billion, the majority, will be excluded. As brothers and sisters, members of our great human family, every one of these people has the potential to be inspired by the need for compassion. And compassion can be developed and nurtured without following or practising a particular religion.

Today, we are faced with many global problems such as poverty, overpopulation and the destruction of the environment. These are problems that we have to address together. No single community or nation can expect to solve them on its own. This indicates how interdependent our world has become. The global economy too is becoming increasingly integrated so that the results of an election in one country can affect the stock market in another. In ancient times, each village was more or less self-sufficient and independent. There was neither the need nor the expectation of cooperation with others outside the village. You survived by doing everything yourself. The situation now has completely changed. It has become very old-fashioned to think only in terms of my nation or my country, let alone my village. Universal responsibility is the real key to overcoming our problems.

Modern India is confronted by many problems. New initiatives and ideas will be required to deal with them. Because of its respected stature and ancient heritage, India has a responsibility not only to ensure the future happiness of its own people, but also to provide leadership in the world. When India was struggling for freedom, individuals who really cared for the welfare of the people came forward at enormous personal sacrifice to take the lead. They possessed the courage and determination to face hardship. Now, may be more than in the past, there is great need for such kinds of dedicated and honest people. It is not a time for such individuals to retire in search of their own narrow happiness. India needs people who can integrate its rich heritage with the modern world, and who have the courage to forgo immediate personal concerns for the greater good. This would indeed be a fitting expression of universal responsibility.

3
Native American Values

PRAVRAJIKA VRAJAPRANA

> Understanding begins with love and respect. It begins with respect for the Great Spirit, and the Great Spirit is the life that is in all things—all the creatures and the plants and even the rocks and the minerals. All things—and I mean all things—have their own will and their own way and their own purpose; this is what is to be respected.
>
> —Rolling Thunder of the Shoshone nation.

'In 1492 Columbus sailed/The ocean blue. . .' Walk into an American elementary school and you can hear a throng of high-pitched voices reciting their nation's history in sing-song enthusiasm, rhythmical cadences teaching the young about Columbus's 'discovery' of America. Unfortunately, it's not true. For Native Americans in particular, the teaching of such 'history' is painful and galling. As one Algonquin Indian quipped, 'We were here about 15,000 years before you showed up.'*

Before the first European ever stepped foot on these shores, great indigenous civilizations had already taken root, flourished, and withered on American soil.[1] When Columbus first viewed this rich, verdant land, the American continents were already nurturing 75,000,000 inhabitants who spoke 2,000 different languages.[2]

Only now are archeologists beginning to discover what Native Americans have always known: 'Our people know that we have been here since the beginning of time,' said one Haida elder. And the oral tradition of the great Lakota nation solemnly declares: 'Since forever have we been here.' By tracing DNA markers, scientists can now verify that Native peoples have inhabited America for at least 40,000, if not 70,000 years.[3] It only makes their history all the more poignant.

> When we were created, we were given our ground to live on and from this time these were our rights. This is all true. We were put here by the Creator—I was not brought from a foreign country and did not come here. I was put here by the Creator.—Chief Weninock of the Yakima nation.

Columbus's arrival on American shores marked the beginning of what eventually became a desperate, unforgiving struggle between two highly developed but mutually

---

* Throughout this article, the terms 'Native American' and 'American Indian' will be used interchangeably. Although 'American Indian' is a flagrant misnomer, it was nevertheless the accepted term until recent years.

antagonistic cultures, European and Native American. The history of Native Americans since that epochal time has been bloody, bitter, sorrowful. Xenophobic and culturally blind, the new European arrivals were incapable of seeing the native inhabitants as anything less than culturally, psychologically, morally, and spiritually inferior. To the Europeans, the Native Americans were less than human; their very existence posed a threat to civilized Christian people. Wherever the white people came, the native population had little choice but to leave or die.

But for the Native Americans, it wasn't a simple question of packing up a suitcase and leaving for a new part of town. For them the earth was sacred; the land on which they lived was deeply connected to their spirituality and to their identity as a people. It could not be owned. 'We did not think we owned the land,' said a Lakota elder. 'It is like talking about owning your grandmother. You can't own your grandmother.' The elder continued:

> Then something happened that we don't understand. The people who came said that we don't belong here anymore. That there was a chief in Washington . . . and the land was his, and he said that they could live here and we could not. We thought they were insane . . . . These people would ride across the land and put a flag up, then say that everything between where they started and where they put the flag up belonged to them . . . . That was like someone shooting an arrow into the sky and saying that all the sky up to where the arrow went belonged to him.[4]

Eventually forced from their sacred lands, Native Americans were either killed, felled by disease, or herded into reservations—de facto concentration camps for American Indians.

'It has been estimated that by the seventeenth century, more than 50 million natives . . . perished as a result of war, disease, enslavement, and the careless or deliberate brutality of Europeans—history's greatest holocaust so far. . . . Among the whites, there was scarcely the blinking of an eye over the devastating impact of the Europeans on an Indian world that had been millennia in the making,' Native American authority Alvin Josephy writes. Between 1860 and 1890 'the culture and civilization of the American Indian was destroyed,' historian Dee Brown observed.[5]

By the middle of the twentieth century, the Native American population had dwindled to a nadir of 250,000 people. Morale was at its lowest ebb; the rate of alcoholism, suicide, and unemployment among the Native Americans was the highest in the country. Hardly surprising since, for the most part, Native Americans lived in squalid reservations—denied the right to govern themselves and manage their own affairs.[6] And, appallingly, until the Freedom of Religion Act of 1978, Native Americans were even denied the right to practise their religion—the ballast and bedrock of Native American life.

Yet today Native American culture—what is left of it after many tribes and languages have become extinct—is showing a profound resurgence. After years of unrelenting oppression, the Native American remains unbowed—a great tree standing proud after a hurricane. Ironically, many non-Natives are now turning to Native American traditions for the spiritual sustenance that contemporary American culture lacks.

What has given these people the strength to endure? Their values. What do these impoverished people possess that the world's richest nation now hungrily seeks? Their enduring spiritual values that have kept a people alive. 'The traditional American Indian,' according to Yellowtail,**

> is an individual who has self-esteem in his sacred way of life, a person who is trying to follow the straight path in everything. He tries to do things right and not be greedy . . . He will want enough to live on, but that is all the Indian cares for. He shares whatever he has been given with his fellow man and does not try to get ahead of others . . . The Indian is not rich in possessing wealth and money. We Indian people are rich in spiritual wealth, which is more important.[7]

What is the sacred way of life for a Native American? It is a way of life that is practised every day of the week, every minute of the day. There is no division between the sacred and the secular. Every aspect of life is *wakan*, sacred. This was especially true before 'civilization' imposed itself on traditional Native American life. 'In the old days my people did not separate daily life in the world from spiritual life,' said Fools Crow.*** 'Everything was spiritual. We were soaked in it. It is only now that we see a difference. Our attitude was spiritual and *Wakan Tanka* [the Lakota word for the Great Spirit] and His Helpers were involved in everything we thought and did.'[8]

** Yellowtail was chief medicine man of the Crow nation until he handed down his authority to John Pretty On Top in 1984. Although quite elderly, Yellowtail participated in the 1993 Chicago Parliament of Religions, and died not long thereafter. On his final day, Yellowtail remained absorbed in prayer and meditation, praying for world peace and the welfare of humanity.

*** Fools Crow was Ceremonial Chief of the Titon Sioux until his death in 1989 at the age of ninety-nine.

Yellowtail of the Crow nation echoes the same thought: 'The Indian knows that even the smallest animal has great importance and can teach us great things. So too, all the little things we do every day have great importance. Our life is full of many little things in each day and in every moment. We should not concentrate on some great event that we expect to come in the future, but on the correct performance of all our daily obligations. In this way, we will show respect for all created things and for *Acbadadea.*'[9]

Acbadadea, Wakan Tanka, Kehce Manitu, and *Taiowa* are, respectively, the Crow, Lakota, Cree, and Hopi tribal names for the Unnamable; they are untranslatable. 'One of the greatest difficulties regarding translation of Native languages in English,' said White Deer of Autumn, 'lies with understanding the Native American concept of a First Cause.' These tribal names 'incorporate an understanding that all things are part of an incomprehensible totality which always was and always will be . . . Terms now commonly used such as God, Creator, and Great Spirit are not adequate names . . . . That is the failure of the English language, not of the idea.'[10]

How, then, can we describe *Wakan Tanka,* the Great Mystery? 'Wakan Tanka is all that is wondrous, awesome, powerful, and infinite, and yet He is also personal, compassionate, loving and tender,' said Pete Catches, the great Lakota medicine chief. 'Perhaps this is why we call him Great Mystery.'[11] The Great Mystery is infinite and inexpressible, yet He possesses all the blessed qualities of the personal God.

When he was in his eighties, Fools Crow suffered very much from a painful arthritic condition in his knees. So advanced was the condition that Fools Crow could stand up and sit down only with the greatest difficulty. In fact, instead of sitting down, he'd simply drop down instead. Seeing this, the Lutheran minister Thomas Mails asked Fools Crow why he didn't heal his own knees—knowing full well that Fools Crow possessed the power to do so. 'Yes,' Fools Crow replied, 'but Wakan Tanka has already been so good to me, I don't have the heart to ask Him for more.'[12]

We can go still further: Wakan Tanka is not only the transcendent God—both personal and impersonal, with and without attributes—He also resides in the human heart. The Oglala Sioux visionary, Black Elk, said, 'The heart is a sanctuary at the centre of which there is a little space, wherein the Great Spirit dwells . . . . In order to know the centre of the heart where the Great Spirit dwells you must be pure and good, and live in the manner that the Great Spirit has taught us. The man who is thus pure contains the universe in the pocket of his heart.'[13] For those of us steeped in the Vedanta tradition, the Native American view of God seems familiar indeed.

How, then, does the Native American view the world? According to Pete Catches, the universe is like a massive design woven by a sacred power, constantly breathed into by the breath of Wakan Tanka.

> People and this world and all that is in it are only a part of Wakan Tanka, the lesser part when you consider the limitlessness of eternity and the universe, and the limits and relative insignificance of matter as we know ourselves and this world to be.
>
> Look at the tiny ants going about their business on the ground in front of us. In this world, everything has its purpose, its time and its place, from the smallest particle to the powerful

> storms as they sweep and wash the face of the land. Men also come and go, but man is different from the ants, for he must learn where his place is and what his life means. That we may do this, our people were given a way of prayer.[14]

Prayer is the central pivot from which Native American values draw their strength. 'Prayer—the daily recognition of the Unseen and the Eternal—is our one inevitable duty,' said Ohiyesa of the Santee Sioux. 'Our daily devotions are more important to us than food.'[15]

There are different kinds of prayer. There is the prayer that greets the day with the rising of the sun: 'After the bath, we stand erect before the advancing dawn, facing the sun . . . and offer our unspoken prayer. Our mate may preceed or follow us in our devotions, but never accompanies us. Each soul must meet the morning sun, the new sweet earth, and the Great Silence alone.'[16] Cree elder Vern Harper observed, 'There's a time in the morning when you don't hear [the birds] chirping, and our belief is that the birds are silent because it's our turn to pray . . . When the birds are silent, then it's our time to pray. That's because everything is connected; everything is related.'[17]

There is the spontaneous prayer that greets beauty throughout the day: 'Whenever, in the course of our day, we might come upon a scene that is strikingly beautiful or sublime . . . we pause for an instant in the attitude of worship.'[18]

There are petitional prayers, prayers for the welfare of others: 'In the prayers that open and close the day,' Yellowtail said, 'we should be praying for everybody and extending our prayers out, covering much more than just praying for certain people. We should be praying for the whole world . . . so that we will live in peace . . . . We should pray that people will see that the answer to their problems is to follow their religion, to pray. We should also realize that God may not answer all our prayers. God knows best, and His ways are not always easy for us to understand.'[19]

There are prayers that accompany the sacred ceremonies: the sweat lodge ceremonies, the sacred pipe, and the Sun Dance, for example. One particularly lovely prayer has been a part of the Sioux sacred tradition for thousands of years: All important ceremonies end with the words *mitakuye oyasin,* which means 'all my relations.' The real meaning behind this simple expression is explained by Janet McCloud, a Tulalip elder: 'When they say . . . *mitakuye oyasin,* all my relatives, it includes everyone who was ever born, or even unborn, in the universe, all the two-legged, the four-legged, birds, animals, rocks, and everyone who's here today. The trees, plants, mountains, sun, moon, stars, and everyone who ever *will* be born! How immense can a statement be? All my relations. I marvel at the beauty of that word, it's so powerful.'[20]

There is also the continual prayer of the heart reaching for the sacred. 'While the prayer with the pipe will start and end the day,' Yellowtail observed,

> it is also important to pray during the day. Each day, whatever I am doing, I am always praying and thinking of God. As I work along . . . I am always praying right along when I am alone . . . All the time I am praying. Acbadadea knows that I pray to Him, and He hears me. I am always praying, no matter what I am doing. I am so used to it that I just can't stop, and I think that it is the best thing a person can do . . . If you look for them, then you will find many parts of the day that could be spent in praying. I am sure that there are a lot of people who are that

> way, continually praying to God, remembering the name of God. For a Crow, 'Acbadadea' is probably the best short prayer during the day. This does great honour to God. Praying for people is also good. Once you get used to that, why, you just can't get away from it . . . People think that other things are more important than prayer, but they are mistaken . . . A person should measure his wealth in terms of the knowledge and love of God.[21]

But can prayer properly be called a Native American value? Yes, because prayer informs and animates all other areas of Native American life. Speaking of Fools Crow, Thomas Mails remembered, 'The old holy man . . . had taught me that the more time you spend and the deeper you go [in meditation, or what Fools Crow calls 'immersion'] the greater the success of your quest. The entire idea has to do with achieving a state of complete communion with *Wakan Tanka.*' Fools Crow then added,

> The amount of time spent in immersion is never wasted, and it reverses the usual procedure we follow . . . . Ordinarily, we think we must rush and organize to get at the work because there is so little time. If we pray at all . . . it is only briefly, because we have so much to do. Then we spend the entire day working on the chores, and end up frustrated and drained. With immersion, you spend a lot of time in prayer, obtain from the Higher Powers the strength and guidance you need, then finish those same chores in a fraction of the time, ending up fulfilled and fresh.[22]

One of the most central values for Native Americans is respect and reverence for all forms of life. This attitude engenders a prayerful attitude, and the prayerful attitude in turn feeds the individual's reverence for creation. Whereas 'civilized' societies have put humanity at the pinnacle of creation at the expense of everything else, Native

Americans have always seen all of creation as a united, sacred whole. The earth—mother to us all—was always accorded the greatest respect along with all created beings.

Human beings are the highest manifestation of God's power, because they alone can know the Wakan Tanka. But all other creatures are also manifestations of the Great Spirit; created before us, they are our elders and deserve respect. 'From Wakan Tanka, the Great Spirit, came a great unifying force that flowed in and through all things,' said Luther Standing Bear,

> the flowers of the plains, blowing winds, rocks, trees, birds, animals—and was the same force that had been breathed into the first man. Thus all things were kindred and were brought together by the same Great Mystery. Kinship with all creatures of the earth, sky, and water was a real and active principle . . . . The animals had rights—the right of man's protection, the right to live, the right to multiply, the right to freedom, and the right to man's indebtedness—and in recognition of these rights the Lakota never enslaved an animal, and spared all life that was not needed for food and clothing.
>
> This concept of life and its relations was humanizing, and gave to the Lakota an abiding love. It filled his being with the joy and mystery of living; it gave him reverence for all life . . . The Lakota could despise no creature for all were . . . made by the same hand, and filled with the essence of the Great Mystery.[23]

Generosity is another value that thc Native American highly esteems. Since we are all connected to one another, the greatest joy and privilege is found in giving whatever one has to others. 'Wakan Tanka's wish is that we do for others,' Fools Crow said. 'Those who live for one another learn that love is the bond of perfect unity. Perfect unity is when you put other people ahead of yourself.'[24] Since generosity is an integral part of a Native American's identity, every Native American celebration or occasion is generally accompanied by a 'giveaway'—giving away one's things to others.

> It has always been our belief that the love of possessions is a weakness to be overcome . . . and if allowed its way it will in time disturb the spiritual balance for which we all strive. Therefore we must early learn the beauty of generosity. As children we are taught to give what we prize most, that we may taste the happiness of giving; at an early age we are made the family giver of alms. If a child is inclined to be grasping, or to cling too strongly to possessions, legends are related that tell of the contempt and disgrace falling on those who are ungenerous and mean.
>
> Public giving is a part of every important ceremony. It properly belongs to the celebration of birth, marriage, and death, and is observed whenever it is desired to do special honour to any person or event. Upon such occasions it is common to literally give away all that one has to relatives, to guests of another tribe or clan, but above all to the poor and the aged, from whom we can hope for no return.
>
> Finally, the gift to the Great Mystery, the religious offering, may be of little value in itself, but to the giver's own thought it should carry the meaning and reward of true sacrifice.[25]

Silence is another value cherished by Native Americans. For this reason they have been called, 'dumb Indians' or 'stone-faced Indians'—not realizing that for Native Americans, needless talk is considered a great weakness of character. Sonny Billie, a Seminole elder said, 'A knowledgeable Indian will often not say too much, and some white folks might mistake this for being dumb. But we were taught not to speak too quickly unless we're sure of what we're saying because words can be like weapons, they can hurt. The white man has lots of words for "I'm sorry." '[26]

'We believe profoundly in silence,' said Ohiyesa, for it is

> the sign of a perfect equilibrium. Silence is the absolute poise or balance of body, mind, and spirit. Those who can preserve their selfhood ever calm and unshaken by the storms of existence . . . . possess the ideal attitude and conduct of life.
>
> If you ask us, 'What is silence?' we will answer, 'It is the Great Mystery. The holy silence is God's voice.'
>
> If you ask, 'What are the fruits of silence?' we will answer, 'They are self-control, true courage or endurance, patience, dignity, and reverence. Silence is the cornerstone of character.'[27]

Silence is deeply connected to truthfulness, and truthfulness is the foundation of Native American honour. 'It does not require many words to speak the truth,' Chief Joseph of the Nez Perce observed. To tell a lie was and is considered the blackest sin: 'Such is the importance of our honour and our word that in the early days, lying was a capital offence. Because we believed that the deliberate liar is capable of committing any crime behind the screen of cowardly untruth and double dealing, the destroyer of mutual confidence was summarily put to death, that the evil might go no further.'[28]

Among the Native Americans, truth has always been seen as the great protector, and any sacrifice was welcomed to protect truth. 'Truth always prevails,' said Rose Augur, a Cree elder, 'no matter how many years it may take. So when a person lives in honesty and truth, you never have any real hardships, because truth is like a medicine, and it's always going to take care of you. No matter how much you get persecuted.'[29]

Rose knows plenty about persecution, as do the rest of Native Americans. Since Columbus sailed the ocean blue, suffering has been the Native American's invariable lot. Yet suffering has always been seen by the Native Americans as a way to honour Wakan Tanka and to serve humanity. Charlotte Black Elk of the Oglala Sioux nation said at the 1993 World's Parliament of Religions in Chicago: 'We believe that we possess our *sichon,* our choice, our power . . . the power to be happy, the power . . . to suffer and the power to know great joy. And *that* we truly own. Because everything material is borrowed from the earth . . . and it belongs to God; you don't give to God what God already owns, and what you simply have use of. And so we give the one thing that we can—we suffer so that nothing else in creation needs to suffer.'

No one can doubt that Native Americans have suffered; their suffering has also been their legacy. The flame of their spirituality has not been extinguished. The force of their character has left their conquerors ashamed and awed.

> Our contribution to our nation and the world is not to be measured in the material realm. Our greatest contribution has been spiritual and philosophical. Silently, by example only . . . we have held stoutly to our native vision . . . . We have not advertised our faithfulness nor made capital of our honour . . . This simplicity and fairness has cost us dear. It has cost us our land and our freedom, and even the extinction of our race as a separate and unique people. But, as an ideal, we live and will live, not only in the splendour of our past . . . . but in the living heart of the nation.[30]

What values can we learn from Native Americans? Fools Crow said that to serve both God and humanity, 'you must love everyone, put others first, be moral, keep your life in order . . . and have a good character.'[31] A Lakota elder told an admiring young white man, 'You want to know how to be like Indians? Live close to the earth. Get rid of some of your things. Help each other. Talk to the Creator. Be quiet more. Listen to the earth instead of building things on it all the time.'[32]

All of us have something that we can learn from Native American values. Mitakuye oyasin.

References

1. Betty and Ian Ballentine, eds., *The Native Americans: An Illustrated History* (Atlanta: Turner Publications, 1993), p. 26.
2. 'Search for the First Americans,' *Nova,* Public Broadcasting System, April 25, 1995.
3. Ibid.
4. Kent Nerburn, *Neither Wolf Nor Dog* (San Rafael, CA: New World Library), p.40, 42.
5. *Bury My Heart at Wounded Knee,* 2d ed. (New York: Holt, Rinehart & Winston, 1971), p. xv.
6. Ballentine, pp. 17–18.
7. Michael Oren Fitzgerald, ed., *Yellowtail: Crow Medicine Man and Sun Dance Chief: An Autobiography* (Norman, OK: University of Oklahoma Press, 1991), p. 8.
8. Thomas E. Mails, *Fools Crow: Wisdom and Power* (Tulsa, OK: Council Oak Books, 1991), p. 50.
9. Fitzgerald, p. 105.
10. Steve Wall and Harvey Arden, *Wisdomkeepers* (Hillsboro, OR: Beyond Words Pub., 1990), p. 4.

11. Arthur Amiotte, 'Eagle Fly Over,' *Parabola,* Vol. 1, Issue 3, Summer 1976, p. 35.
12. Mails, p. 25.
13. Fitzgerald, p. 105.
14. Ibid., p. 29.
15. Kent Nerburn, ed. *The Soul of an Indian: And Other Writings from Ohiyesa* (San Rafael, CA: New World Library, 1993), pp. 7, 9.
16. Ibid., p. 9.
17. Sandy Johnson, ed., *The Book of Elders: The Life Stories and Wisdom of Great American Indians* (New York: HarperCollins, 1994), p. 127.
18. Ibid., pp. 9–10.
19. Fitzgerald, p. 127.
20. Johnson, p. 60.
21. Ibid., pp. 126–27.
22. Mails, p. 32.
23. Kent Nerburn and Louise Mengelkoch, eds., *Native American Wisdom* (San Rafael,CA: New World Library, 1991), pp. 43–44.
24. Mails, p. 52.
25. *Soul of an Indian,* pp. 23–24.
26. Johnson, pp. 177–78.
27. Ibid., pp. 3–4.
28. Ibid., p. 36.
29. Johnson, p. 139.
30. *Soul of an Indian,* pp. 59–60.
31. Mails, p. 42.
32. *Neither Wolf Nor Dog*. p. 161.

4
Values of the Sadhu

SWAMI VIDYATMANANDA

The American writer Edith Wharton is reported to have said, 'I don't believe in God, but I do believe in His saints.'

At first glance, an apparently flippant statement, but understandable upon mature reflection. You have only to think about it to see that Edith Wharton's is a sentiment with which many would agree. The concept of God is remote—available mainly through scriptural reports and the claims of theology. But the concrete evidence of living, functioning saintliness—which we can see in an occasional advanced human being—is immediately believable and powerfully convincing. Such human saintliness may be the best and only Godliness that some of us are capable of perceiving—the Ultimate being more available through his saintly particularities than through Itself! Godly qualities manifested in a human being offer the best demonstration of the God that we cannot otherwise see. For most of us, a living, functioning saint is more precious than a divine concept sought mainly through an effort of imagination.

Thus the enormous value of His Saints, of which a primary example is what we call a *sadhu*—a holy man (or woman) whom we are occasionally fortunate to find in our midst. In Vedanta the word *sadhu* is a general term meaning spiritual person. The word comes from the Sanskrit *sadh,* a verb meaning 'to lead to fulfilment.' He (or she) is very holy and at the same time reassuringly human.

I have known and worked with a real sadhu. And for this experience I shall be grateful forever. I don't say that I don't believe in God, as Edith Wharton says she does not, but like her I find the Divine more easily accessible in His saints. My conception of Sadhu Values comes from this experience—what qualities I saw manifested in my sadhu. I shall try to give a description in such a way as to reveal what these values are, expressed in him.

The primary quality I would cite is *availability*. My sadhu was open to everybody whether they were easy and attractive or not. He once told me that he had at a certain moment decided to make as many friends during his lifetime as possible, and he made good his intention. My sadhu had developed a sunny, permissive personality; one sensed that one could unguardedly tell him anything and that he would be interested. Moreover he would not judge or condemn, and he would keep one's confidences. Although being essentially of a shy disposition and unassertive in most fields of activity, my sadhu was uncharacteristically aggressive in attracting and cultivating new contacts. He was especially interested in those individuals having adjustment difficulties—the misfits, the friendless, the inept. And how they did respond to his advances! I teased him by labelling him an obsessive collector of wounded birds.

Besides having to conduct continual personal interviews, my sadhu's availability resulted in an enormous correspondence—long and complicated recitations of personal problems expressed in difficult handwritings and several languages. Once when my sadhu confessed that he was overwhelmed by the flow of letters I reminded him that his ambition had been to acquire as many friends as possible. 'Here is your result!' I asked him what it was that all those people wrote about. His answer was: 'It's very simple. They want to tell somebody something that is interesting to them, and they assume that that something is interesting to the person to whom they are writing. So I try to reply, even a few lines. Generally not giving advice, but just being friendly and encouraging. It gives them comfort.'

I had thus a daily demonstration of something my own guru tried to inculcate in me and which I was so slow to learn: 'Feel for others, my child,' he often entreated. 'You must learn to feel for others.'

The second Sadhu Value my sadhu adhered to was *positiveness.* He genuinely believed in the potential perfectability of everyone. The quality of not criticizing was firmly established as a part of his personality. When someone did something clearly unwise or obviously wrong, his usual observation was: 'But he's like that, that's his nature. What can he do?' And then he would probably add, 'But he will surely change.' That's the final line of the few negative assessments of people I ever heard my sadhu utter: 'He will suffer from the course he is taking, and suffering will force him to change.' How many times I heard these words from him! 'He (or she) will surely change.' He never looked at people according to the weaknesses which they manifested at a given time. Rather, he considered them as, certainly not bad, but merely immature. He believed in the future spiritual success of everybody he came in contact with, and it was this belief in them that attracted so many people to him.

Try as I did, I could never manage to involve my sadhu in the behavioural shortcomings of others in the community. Any complaint was turned aside blandly. 'Moods change.' His policy when he was himself scolded or complained against was to remain silent. Just to sit silently until the other had run out of words. So no self-defence, just silence. This response had the effect of disarming the assailant and finally forcing him to desist, defeated. My sadhu was impossible to quarrel with. Once, however, when I was really irritated about something he had done I made up my mind to 'have things out' with him. He listened in silence to my angry words and then answered calmly: 'You know you are angry. So your reason is disturbed. We'll wait a little while for the emotion to go and then we'll discuss the matter like the good friends we are.'

I see now that only a saintly man—a sadhu—could act in the ways I have described. The early uncertainty I felt in dealing with a man so different from anyone I had ever met before turned into admiration—even emulation. I tried to learn to follow the same modes of behaviour myself. 'Be patient, be positive, and let things work out. Who can tell what is good, what is ultimately bad, what is progress, what is success? It all depends. Progress is so individual. Don't come to conclusions. There are so many criteria, spiritual unfoldment is too subtle to analyze. Who knows how God works? Who knows what God wants?'

For my sadhu the purpose of religion was to produce a change in the individual who practised it—a change of character, a change in his habitual reactions, a fundamental change in that person's very thought-patterns. A genuinely spiritual person is one who has learned to live at peace with oneself, who lives in peace with others, and who copes competently with the vagaries of the everyday world in which human beings are forced to live. My sadhu was not impressed by claims concerning mystical experiences or celestial emotions when not accompanied by a corresponding amelioration in the individual's life-style. 'Have you become a mature person?' would have been his question. Spiritual practice, properly done, should transform an individual into something of a sage, as it had transformed him.

I have said that the Sadhu Values which I beheld in my sadhu were *availability* and *positiveness*. He practised them conscientiously, and his effect on those fortunate to know him was generative. For many individuals my sadhu was the only God they cared to know, the grace he transmitted was sufficient for them. Whether or not they would be able ultimately to believe in God as God, in any case they had His Saint as preinstructor. We may suppose that these Sadhu Values were God's means of bringing those lovers of my sadhu eventually to Himself.

5
Values in Family

NIVEDITA R. BHIDE

If we analyse any problem in the world, we reach the conclusion that the root cause of it is we ourselves. If we humans had been self-effacing, less greedy, and more considerate toward our own species as well as toward other species and Nature, then there would have been no problem. This discussion about the need for values in our life invariably takes us to the values in the family, because our life can be shaped best in an environment that a family with values provides.

In the Indian social system the unit of society is not an individual but a family. Traditionally, every person's life is divided into four stages. In the second stage, called Grihasthashrama, a person takes to family life and is expected to serve society. Our forefathers, the rishis, had conscientiously set the family on firm foundations so as to ensure the stability of society. It is this admirable family system which led many historians to comment that the law and order, culture, and personal virtues did not suffer in India even under foreign rule or in times of war.

The principle which predominantly ruled in the family was dharma, a word which defies definition in English. 'Family' does not mean a group of people related to each other by law or blood and living together. It is a social unit with a definite purpose—namely, man-making and nurturing of society. The 'Five Great Sacrifices' (*pañca- mahāyajña*), which every householder is expected to perform, illustrate beautifully how the values for self-unfoldment as well as for the care of society and Nature were made a part of daily life.

Brahma-Yajña or *Ṛṣi-Yajña*. This involves studying what the rishis had discovered through contemplation about the different aspects of life, interpreting their teachings in modern terms, and adding to them new insights out of our own authentic experiences, in order to pass them on to the succeeding generations. So Ṛṣi-yajña is a very vast yajña which every thinking person should perform. Our service to the mother-land, specially at the thought-level, should be such that the philosophy of life which India has evolved over the millennia should be understood and this 'Indianness' should not be lost in the zeal for modernization.

Not only that but, as Swami Vivekananda envisaged, India should be equipped to give her message of spirituality to the whole world. Thus the mission of the nation is fulfilled by the family. When a family is aware of the good that accrues by these things, values become an integral part of our life. For that, the householder should be well acquainted with the rishis through regular studies of their works, pilgrimages and by interacting with those who live in villages and forests.

Also, we should devote daily some time to chant scriptural texts and hymns which tell us that the whole universe is pervaded by God and therefore each soul is potentially divine. We may contemplate for some time on the divine nature of our true self and on the interconnectedness of the universe. Then we must pray for the welfare of all.

Pitṛ-Yajña. An essential feature of a family is the respect that its elders are given. Pitṛ-yajña embodies the respect given and the service rendered to parents, teachers and other elders, and also to our ancestors.

Deva-Yajña. 'Deva' here refers to those deities who preside over our sense-organs and also the deities who represent different forces of Nature. Deva-yajña in the present context means, first, those acts or exercises which make our body strong and intellect sharp. Secondly, it also means that we should keep our surroundings clean and work towards the preserving of the ecological balance.

Bhūta-Yajña. Animals, birds and plants form an essential part in human life. Like ourselves they too are God's creation. Caring for them and living in harmony with the external nature constitute Bhuta-Yajña.

Nṛ-Yajña. This is the yajña to Sri Narayana, or God, present in Nara, or human being. It is a worship offered to Sri Narayana, who manifests Himself in us all—and particularly in the poor, the ignorant and the suffering. To do this yajña, we should set apart at least some money and an hour everyday. If that is not possible, at least five hours should be devoted every week to serve the poor, the fallen, and the downtrodden.

Family is an institution. An institution can function effectively only if it follows the rule of continuity and change. The entry of a newly-wed bride into the house of her husband is an important landmark in any family. She is the child of the present and represents 'change' whereas the in-laws, the products of the past, represent 'continuity'. The in-laws act as the link connecting the past to the present. They ensure continuity in a family. Both the bride and the in-laws have to understand and love each other to allow an uninterrupted progress in the family. The holding together or the breaking apart of a family generally gets decided at this point, namely, the entry of a daughter-in-law.

In our tradition, the wife is called a Saha-dharmacāriṇī, meaning, one who practises dharma along with her husband. This dharma includes the traditions of her new family. How she treats her parents-in-law is usually a good indication of how her children will treat her when she gets old. For the parents-in-law, the bride is Lakshmi incarnate of the house. If they want their family to prosper—if they want peace, happiness, and wealth for the family—they have to keep her happy. If she is unhappy, the whole household gets disturbed. It is through mutual understanding and loving care that the highest good in any family is attained.

Sister Nivedita describes vividly in her book *Web of Indian Life* how, for the young bride, the husband is not only a person but the whole household. So taking care of him means caring for each and every member of the family. Self-effacement at its maximum by each, at his or her level, lends sweetness to the family. The more everyone becomes individualistic, the more there is of fragmentation of not only the family but, ultimately, of even the minds and personalities of the family members. That is why in America, where 66% of the children are now of single parent, crime is on the rise. Even their political parties are so alarmed that in their manifesto they stress the importance of family, even making legislations for tax-exemption to every husband and wife living together. In India, of course, 'family' does not mean only children and parents living together, but it includes grandparents, aunts, and uncles also. Any person getting a job amounts to the whole family getting it, as the benefit goes to everyone in the family. There are instances of a brother or a sister staying unmarried till some others in the family are settled properly in life. Nearly 250 million of our people will be on the streets if Indians decide to be individualistic and to take care of only their own wife and children.

The purpose of a family is to establish dharma in society by creating dhārmic prajā. The word used for children born out of lust is *santati*. But the children begotten with prayers are called *prajā*. Lasting values can be inculcated into children only through two methods: one, personal example and, two, intense and yet restrained love.

For children, their parents are the examples to follow. Children never learn through lectures and the do's and don'ts given by their parents. They learn by *observing* the parents. When their mother keeps aside everything to watch a movie on TV, her little ones understand that seeing movies is the most important work. If their father uses his office stationery for personal use, the children unconsciously learn the lesson of corruption. If elders in a family idle away their weekends, the children think that is what relaxing means.

I remember how my father inculcated in his children the habit of reading good books. He encouraged us to be members of a public library and left the choice of books to be read entirely to us. When I brought a good book, he too would go through it. At dinner time he would speak about the book brought by me. If I brought home from the library some novel not worth reading, he would look at it and keep it aside, saying that it was not a good one. Sometimes he would remark that the author made only soft dolls out of young people. He neither lectured me as to which books should be read nor rebuked me for bringing bad books, but his silent message and encouragement for bringing good books was so effective that, unknown to myself, I developed a taste for good books.

If the parents quarrel for the sake of their own desires and comforts, the children learn to be selfish. The goal of life decides the quality and the texture of life. Our ultimate goal is God-realisation, or the attainment of oneness with the whole universe. When this goal is clear to the elders in the family, their behaviour naturally reflects the cherished values, and these are automatically imbibed by children. If the goal of life is limited to earning only money and status, then the selfish behaviour of the elders gets multiplied in geometric progression in their children.

Children always observe their parents: how they behave with each other, with elderly members in the family, with neighbours, with servants, etc. Thus the norms of all relationships are taught and learnt in the family. Parents cannot avoid this method of teaching values. By the very nature of the family, the parents are the first people children get to know and so the children observe them and imbibe their traits. This education is unavoidable. If the parents expect their children to develop as wholesome personalities, their own lives must be wholesome and exemplary. My mother used to do morning chores chanting the patriotic poems of Veer Savarkar. She never lectured to her children on patriotism but we are all intensely patriotic, because we have seen day after day that our mother chose to remember Veer Savarkar every morning through his poems.

The second method by which children imbibe values is by intense but restrained love showered on them. In today's materialistic world, love is often equated with material goods. The parents think that the best way to express or show their love is to give the children whatever they fancy or demand. Rarely do such indulgent parents say no to their children. This spoils the children so much that by the time the parents find that their grown-up children have gone completely out of control, it is usually too late to restrain them. All the sermonizing about the do's and don'ts falls on deaf years at that stage.

The parents must learn to say a firm no to their children's demands so as to train them for life where they are never going to get everything they desire. Children actually like to be disciplined by their parents, but this becomes possible only if parents spend their time with them and not just money. Taking daily at least a meal together, celebrating together some of the festivals, explaining to the children the purpose of those festivals, doing household errands together, reading some good books together, having at least once a week a bhajan or prayer session—these are some of the ways to spend time fruitfully with children. Our festivals are occasions not only for learning about our culture but also when we can relate ourselves meaningfully to society and to Nature. How effectively, genuinely, and lovingly parents can make use of the festivals to teach values to their children! But, alas, as money is increasingly becoming the ruling deity of our life, the elders in a family usually discuss only the perks or bonus they would get or the new dresses to be purchased.

Ultimately we see that striving for values in a family—either through the way of the 'Five Great Sacrifices' or as consideration for others—results in a gradual self- transformation of every family-member. India is a spiritual nation. Many Eastern as well as Western savants have envisaged that she has a mission to spiritualize the world. In order to fulfil that mission, India must strengthen herself and that process of strengthening is possible only by re-vitalizing our family system.

6

Three Points of View

HEDI AND NIK BOESTEN

We are a family of four living in Germany: the husband is employed at the provincial government of Schleswig-Holstein, the wife is a part-time primary school-teacher, the son and daughter are sixteen and eleven years of age respectively. We married late in life and adopted two children from India. Before we decided to do this, we met an elderly teacher of Hatha Yoga and, through her, found our way in the mid-eighties to Swami Ritajananda, the head of the Centre Vedantique in Gretz near Paris. By undertaking this adoption we wanted to do some social service instead of spending our double-income just on ourselves.

Western society is, on the one hand, calling more and more into question family values in practice, not least of all in the context of equality and equal rights for women—and, for instance, provides public care for children from the age of three in kindergartens. There is, on the other hand, a growing propensity towards violence among young people in the West, which experts attribute to the neglect of children in families now threatened with inner conflicts.

If we ask ourselves what the existing family values mean against the spiritual background of Vedanta philosophy, we see that there are three points of view: the point of view of the parents, the point of view of the growing children, and the point of view of society.

Parents' Point of View

If a man and woman marry for love, they are not in perfect harmony in thought and emotion right from the start. Instead, they want to accept one another just as they are, with different developments, and if possible complement one another. From then on, they should bear all responsibilities, perform duties and take decisions together and each can rely on the other. This helps enormously in coping with difficulties at work and in everyday life.

At the same time a process of mutual maturing begins: giving in, showing consideration, accepting the common fate, and giving up selfish desires. This takes place all the more quickly, the earlier the desire for children arises. Then selfless service is required. It culminates in the recognition of the fact that during the children's stay of about twenty years with the family, they are merely given into the care of their parents and that parents must learn to release them unconditionally when the time comes.

In this way humility, contentment and kindness can grow—and in old age, wisdom, which we in our childhood so appreciated in the older generation.

Today the problem for parents in the West is that children are increasingly questioning the traditional family values. They no longer just want to take them over by way of obedience, but accept them only when they have understood their relevance and value after a period of time and a maturing process. Often the only help is if the parents have patiently and constantly set an example and are open to questions, even to have themselves called into question.

From the point of view of the parents, the special value of the family today lies in helping the growing generation to develop and expand healthy and stable self-confidence, teaching them to be responsible and self-critical, and setting an example in the religious conviction that everything is meaningful. From the latter arises an avoidance of too pessimistic thoughts about the future and an inner tranquillity, perhaps even a cheerful prevailing mood.

Growing Children's Point of View

Young people today have to experience their own limitations by adjusting to the community and learning to exercise self-restraint. This starts in the family, continues in kindergarten and school, and also applies in all recreational groups. It is therefore an advantage if there is a sibling in the family. In this way mutual helpfulness, protection of the weak, ability to share, even a sense of justice can be experienced, as these will be essential in the subsequent stages of life and in basic social structures for the sake of peaceful coexistence.

As the children grow up, friends will visit the family circle and find hospitality and tolerance there. The parents then assume more and more the role of companions of their children, of the fatherly friend and motherly adviser. In discussions with these young critical observers, differences get sorted out which the young people may notice in comparing the parents' opinions with their daily behaviour.

Some followers of Vedanta find it difficult to preserve inner quietness in the growing occupational stress in the West, and reconcile their own desire for silence outside working-hours and the understandable wish of the young people for amusement, celebrations, parties and experiences.

Society's Point of View

It is a fact, shown by the destruction of nations and empires, that societies remain intact as long as families are intact. Certain social changes, not necessarily harmful, are of course inevitable with the passage of time. A change we have seen in recent times is the one from the extended family to the nuclear family. This change began after the Second World War due to the housing shortage. But the close contact between the two generations comprising the nuclear family and the grandparents and uncles and aunts remained. The social value of the family thus still represents the scene of peaceful coexistence between the generations.

It makes it crystal clear to the growing children that blood-relationship is the basic principle of human society, and in the event of a serious illness of an older member of the family the younger generation should care for them as also for handicapped family members, before calling on government assistance. The family in its turn bears the responsibility, on behalf of society, for appropriately training and raising the younger generation. Every child should receive adequate care in the family and education until it goes out to work. This is why family-planning or birth-control is a rule in the West.

In this connection we would like to emphasize one important point. It is high time that in the affluent Western society the work of the housewife is recognized, generally respected, and appropriately rewarded as work which can be compared to a profession. The loving care of the children by the mothers, who consequently give up professional work, will then give satisfaction and self-esteem to young women. Young people will no longer have to escape from broken families into groups with a propensity to violence, in order to draw attention to their spiritual needs.

Let us sum up: it is our strong conviction that only a person who is prepared to make a committed contribution for future generations should be allowed to criticize social development in the West. For this purpose there are numerous opportunities for selfless and voluntary commitments. But it is surely also clear that personal willingness and preparedness to serve will not be enough. Without faith in a divine providence it will not work and, in the long run, it'll also need the encouragement of like minded friends. We get both these during our frequent visits to the Ramakrishna Order's ashram in Gretz.

7
Home, Sweet Home

AASHA REDDY

It had been a long and hot day at the office for Aravind. Everything appeared to be going wrong since he started work in the morning. He had an argument with a colleague on trivials, he could not locate some important files in time and, moreover, he had developed a headache. He was longing for the day to be over, because at the end of it was something he could look forward to with pleasure—his home, sweet home.

School was something Divya always enjoyed going to, but today was an exception. She was pulled up by her teacher for something she had not done, her best friend simply ignored her, and she was feeling miserable. Finally, it was the last bell, and with a sense of relief Divya packed up her bag. There was something she could look forward to with pleasure—her home, sweet home.

What is it that makes a home a *sweet* home? Is it the beautiful exterior, the garden, the nice furniture, kitchen gadgets? No, it is people—the parents, the elders, the children and the pets—who make a home sweet. It is the warmth, intimacy and laughter they share that brings joy and happiness into a home. But this kind of harmony does not come about automatically. It needs effort, mutual respect, and a willingness to share common interests, sympathies and pleasures. In other words, it needs the observance of a value system.

According to A. J. Cronin, the famous British author, 'Through the centuries the family has taken foremost place, not only in the safeguarding of morality, but in the evolution of human culture. Wherever the family flourishes in a state of vigour and unity, there will be found a strong and sound society. In an era of fear and restlessness, when people ringed by hostile forces feel isolated in a dark loneliness, the family is their main hope for self-preservation, for maintaining human dignity and the decencies of life.'

Perhaps the most important value a family has to cherish is integrity. It is impossible to imagine any liveable society, let alone a family, without it. Put simply, integrity demands that we always mean what we say and say what we mean, and that we do not cheat or lie to one another. It implies that the affection we profess for anything is genuine and the praise we give is honest. It is a quality which has to be inculcated in children while they are still small. This is something that cannot be taught, but has to be shown. We teach integrity by the way we live ourselves. A small boy was wrongly accused by his teacher of telling a lie. The boy retorted proudly, 'Our family doesn't lie.' Integrity gives one the strength to walk through life with one's head held high.

Children are great imitators and have a natural tendency to do as their parents do. This places a heavy responsibility on parents to lead their lives in such a way that they are talking, walking examples of a set of values which they wish to impart to their children. Many are the times when children are told not to tell lies, but the very next moment they are confused to find their parents asking them to tell a caller that they are not at home. Isn't it a common experience to hear a child say, 'My father told me to tell you that he is not at home'?

There is only one real magic in this life that can move mountains and turn dreams into reality. That magic is 'Believing in yourself.' Only those who believe in themselves and in their capacity to meet challenges are able to face life with courage. Almost anyone can achieve anything if only he believes in himself.

Austrian tennis player Thomas Muster won the French Open title in 1995. He was also acknowledged as the best clay-court player of the year. A few years earlier, he was involved in a serious accident and medical opinion was that he might not be able to walk, let alone play tennis. But through sheer grit, determination and self-effort, he bounced back to the top of his profession. In the words of Swami Vivekananda, 'The old religions said that he was an atheist who did not believe in God. The new religion says that he is an atheist who does not believe in himself.'

Can parents really do anything to encourage self-reliance in a child? Yes, the secret lies in watching to see where a child's innate skills or talents lie and gently nurturing them. We should listen lovingly and respectfully to a child's plans and hopes, however naïve they may seem and, wherever possible, help to make them come true.

Kahlil Gibran, the well-known Lebanese mystic, has expressed this so beautifully in his masterpiece, *The Prophet:*

> You may give them [your children] your love but not your thoughts.
>
> You may house their bodies but not their souls.
>
> For their souls dwell in the house of tomorrow, which you cannot visit, not even in your dreams.
>
> You may strive to be like them, but seek not to make them like you.
>
> For life goes not backward nor tarries with yesterday. You are the bows from which your children as living arrows are sent forth.

Today's children are exposed to many anxiety-causing experiences and caught amidst too many choices. When your daughter comes to you with her fears, listen to her and assure her that it is all right to be scared and that she is not alone in feeling this way. Then help her constructively to overcome them. Making fun of her in such situations can cause irreparable harm. Childhood fears are a part of growing up.

Pessimism, fear and gloom are highly contagious. In a home filled with these, a child's self-confidence can hardly grow or even survive. If however the atmosphere at home is one of love, contentment and laughter, the child develops the ability to look past dark times to brighter ones, to believe that questions do have answers, that challenges can be met, and that problems can be solved. This builds character and endurance, and so the uncertainties of life appear less frightening.

A bit of humour is almost indispensable and helps bring family and friends closer. Humour can help relieve tension and give a new perspective to an otherwise grim and hopeless situation. It enables us, even in trying times, to smile and wink at life.

Open your child's life to the world of books. Read to your young son or daughter at least for a few minutes everyday. Is it hard, in a day packed with 24 hours, to spend at least 15 or 20 minutes to read to your child? Get your child hooked on to reading and he or she will never be alone again.

Children are naturally sensitive to pain and suffering in others. If the climate in the home is one of compassion and concern for others, this sensitivity gets strengthened. We celebrate the birthdays of our children with great enthusiasm and expense. How wonderful it would be if on the same day some money is also spent on fulfilling the needs of the less fortunate!

We spend so much of our time having 'a good time' that we become insensitive to the needs of others. Taking your little son on a monthly visit to an orphanage, any home for the less privileged, or animal shelters will expose him to the values of compassion, love and sharing. Such experiences have the most subtle, profound and enduring influence upon the physical, moral and emotional health of the child. He will experience the joy of giving and sharing and will develop the capacity to love and to feel.

There is a tendency among some women today to downplay the role of a traditional mother in favour of a career. We should be aware, however, that there are many women who enjoy being a wife and mother, not because they are incompetent to pursue a career, but because they derive greater satisfaction from these. According to C. E. Barker, an analytical psychotherapist, 'One of the tragedies of this modern science-soaked society with its obsession for technology, is that mothers now tend to think their contribution to the world is of little account... It assumes that motherhood is a temporary affliction imposed on woman which severely interferes with her fight to show herself as good as man... Alas, such women have no idea that the job of being a mother and offering a tiny human being her identity, warmth, protective love and tenderness, determines the health, well-being, security, stability and sanity of the coming generation.'

Barker continues, 'A generation of good "mothering" would make an unbelievable contribution toward producing a civilization that would work for stability and peace.'

Swami Vivekananda sums up the greatness of motherhood in simple words: 'The position of the mother is the highest in the world, for it is the one place in which to learn and exercise the greatest unselfishness.'

One of the most reassuring and stabilizing experiences in a child's life is the deep love and friendship between the parents. The best way for a father to convey his affection to his children is through the love and understanding he gives to their mother and vice versa. A child's expectations from a father are simple—love and time. What children most remember about their father is his simple presence.

The greatest gift that parents can give to a child is a sense of discipline. Children will benefit by discipline only when it is exacted fairly and firmly and against a background of love. Studies have shown that adults who had been punished in childhood look back in anger, whereas those who had been disciplined look back with gratitude.

A respect for life, for time—ours and that of others—a respect for law, traffic rules, public-property, an awareness of the importance of a clean, green and healthy environment are essential values which need to be implanted in the minds of children, with parents as prime examples. For instance, it is a common sight in Germany to see this signboard at pedestrian crossings: 'Cross only by greenlight: set an example to your children.'

In our daily lives, routine as they may seem, we are very often touched by rare and charming things. The sweetness lies in being able to recognize and appreciate them. We should be able to appreciate little gestures of kindness and the simple beauty of things around us. And above all, the world is about people and the only way you can mean anything to another human being is to share her feelings and yours, and show her that you care. All our feelings, appreciation and good intentions don't mean a thing unless we express them.

Our lives will be so much richer and fuller if we remain young, in the sense that the child within us is never lost. We should grow in all the traits of a child—questioning, curiosity, appreciation, laughter, open-mindedness.

It is not the years but attitudes that make a person seem young or old.

The most precious legacy that we can pass on to our children is a strong religious faith, a belief that there exists a loving God, who cares for us and is ever available to support and help us in times of need. It is the trust that God never abandons us and even in the darkest hour His light still shines to lead us on. This inner conviction will give our children great strength and keep them going in moments of crises.

It is not human society alone which has a value system. There is a particular kind of rodent in Scandinavia called the Lemming. Lemmings live on top of mountains. Whenever there is an abnormal increase in their population leading to shortage of food, a certain number of them run down the mountains and drown themselves in the sea. This is witnessed by a large number of people year after year. Scientists are baffled at this remarkable phenomenon. It can be explained only by assuming that the Lemmings respect the value of self-sacrifice and concern for fellow creatures. We are equally amazed at the social structure and order exhibited by the ants and the bees, which would not be possible without a value system of their own. We humans should be humble enough to recognize this fact and try to emulate them for a harmonious living.

8

Values in Our Education

SWAMI GAUTAMANANDA

Values in our education is a hotly debated subject nowadays. This is because of the chaotic conditions observed in almost all spheres of our national life. It is conjectured, not without reason, that this chaos is mainly due to *lack of values* in the education being imparted in India. This was formulated, as is well-known, by Macaulay in 1836 more to enslave the Indian mind than to liberate it, so that Indians would remain loyal to British Raj, being alienated from their native Vedic culture, education and Sanskrit language. As planned, this gradually weaned our intellectuals away from our classical heritage and from the Sanskrit language, in which lay all our spiritual, cultural, social, and political traditions. We lost our indigenous system of education in which hearing, chanting and memorizing played a great part, assimilation of ideas took place through a well-planned life of service to teacher, contemplation and meditation, all under his guidance. Thus the educated ones in that system were men who had not only knowledge but also character. Knowledge had become a part of their life, influencing their thoughts, emotions and actions. Swami Vivekananda, the prophet-patriot, has said that education is not the amount of information that is put into the brain running riot there, but it is the assimilation of ideas. He also said that education should give us character that would make us flower into the best of humans—full of love, self-confidence, self-reliance, fearlessness, compassion, and a spirit of service like a Buddha, a Christ, or a Ramakrishna. To Swamiji education meant transformation of life from instinctual to intellectual to intuitional level. He was thus advocating the essence of the Vedic values in our education.

Values in Education—What Are They

What are these Vedic values in education? The Sanskrit for values is dharma or Sadācāra. Dharma is described as 'the set of values that sustains the creation without which the very existence of it would be threatened.'[1] Sankaracharya defined dharma as the values that sustained human beings and helped them to enjoy happiness both in this as well as in the spiritual world.

Thus education in India meant not merely intellectual cramming of information into the brain but the application

1. धारणात् धर्म इत्याहुः धर्मो धारयते प्रजाः ।

of them into one's life so that life became better at individual, social, secular, and spiritual levels. Education was a life-transformer. That is real education which liberates.[2]

Thirst for Knowledge

Education was called Vidyā, i.e., acquisition of knowledge, which was compulsory for every boy after he attained the school-going age. Social milieu created this thirst for learning. In the *Chāndogya Upaniṣad* the famous Satyakāma, a boy of school-going age, tells his mother Jabala, 'Mother, I want to go and study under a teacher. Let me know my ancestry (so that I may tell the teacher if asked).'[3] The extant system was to live with an enlightened teacher and to learn all he could teach. This was called the Gurukula system.

Knowledge at Two Levels

What were the subjects a student learnt? We read in the *Muṇḍaka Upaniṣad* the teacher recounting the subjects: All the four Vedas, the science of phonetics, civil engineering, grammar, etymology, poetry, and astronomy. This is only the lower knowedge (*aparā-vidyā*). Quite distinct from this is the higher knowledge, (*parā-vidyā*) 'through which one realizes one's own imperishable soul.'[4]

Thus the Vedic system of education taught knowledge at two levels—one, about the things concerning the world of senses, i.e., almost all known sciences, humanities, arts and

---

2. सा विद्या या विमुक्तये ।

3. ब्रह्मचर्यं भवति विवत्स्यामि किं गोत्रो नु अहमस्मीति—*Ch.Up.*, 4.4.1

4. यया तदक्षरम् अधिगम्यते ।—*Mu.Up.*, 1.1.5

crafts of the times. The second, about Brahman, the divinity which is the material stuff of all creation, the so-called material which was not matter but infinite and immortal pure consciousness. It is from Brahman that all this creation has come, in Brahman it lives, and to Brahman it returns during dissolution.[5] It is this Brahman again that is the soul of man and of all beings. Every student has to learn this at the higher stage of education called Parā-vidyā. Education was considered not complete until both the stages were completed. It was not enough if the student knew only about sciences, arts, engineering or technology. True, this knowledge gave him control over the things and powers of nature. But power without a control-system cannot be safely put to use. What is this control system in man which can make him apply his knowledge *only to useful purposes and never otherwise?* It is his character and culture, which he acquires through Parā-vidyā, the higher knowledge. The higher knowledge teaches that one universal soul permeates all beings, that the individual soul is a part of this universal soul, and hence the individual and the collective (society) are not separate entities but one whole. Hence for a man of right knowledge, love of fellow beings would come as naturally as breathing to the lungs, because he feels that all beings and himself are one in the Universal Self. We know that all limbs are interlinked through the body and any harm to one limb would harm the other limbs too. Thus love, compassion and service to humanity flow as a natural character of a really educated

---

5. यतो वा इमानि भूतानि जायन्ते, येन जातानि जीवन्ति, यत्प्रयन्त्यभिसंविशन्ति ।
—*Tai. Up.*, 3.1.1

man. This constitutes his wisdom. He imbibes these 'values' from a good education.

Values through Education

Thus the 'Science of Spirituality,' as one may call Parā-vidyā, is the power to check and control that comes to man by which all his powers derived from the knowledge of sciences and technology are channelized *only* to welfare purposes of humanity. Such a wise one would never use an atom for destruction, or wealth for enslavement of others, or army for destruction of innocent people. This is the value-system derived through a complete education comprising of Parā and Aparā vidyās.

Concentration

We know what important role the concentration of mind plays in mastering the various subjects of study. The more the power of concentration, the deeper is the observation, the greater is the knowledge gained, and the quicker is it achieved. Hence concentration of mind is a great value stressed in education. Arjuna, the great archer-prince in the epic *Mahābhārata,* is asked to shoot the eye of a bird sitting on a far off tree. He shoots successfully only when he does not see anything else but only the bird's eye. Real concentration cuts off all other objects of senses except the one under observation. Swami Vivekananda's life abounds in examples wherein we see his marvellous power of studying volumes of books by reading them only once and that too with a lightning speed.

Chastity

Concentration can come only to a pure mind. Purity of mind means a mind free from desires and distractions. Desires are of two categories—gross and subtle. Gross ones are those concerning enjoyments of sense-pleasures and the subtle ones are for name, power and position. The sex enjoyment is the leader in the 'gross' category. Therefore to control the sex desire is equivalent to controlling all other desires. Hence the purity of mind much depends on how much the student can observe chastity. The Indian education suggests various methods to sublimate the sex desire through proper attitudes of respect and worshipfulness towards the member of the opposite sex. Through meditation on the divine self in oneself and in others, the identification with one's physical body is replaced by the feeling of oneself as the Atman, which is beyond all sex and form. This, aided by healthy engagements in duties, deep studies and contemplation, enables the student to remain established in chastity to a great degree. Chastity heightens the grasping and retention of knowledge. The student can memorize all he hears from the teachers. Thus concentration and assimilation of ideas are the main features of education. It dispenses with the huge equipments—notebooks, textbooks, work-books, and what not!

Truthfulness

Now comes another great value on which great stress is laid. That is truthfulness. We read in the *Taittirīya Upaniṣad* that after the completion of education, the teacher advises the outgoing students thus: 'Speak the truth, practise dharma, never deviate from study, help the teacher through wealth in his mission of diffusion of knowledge, and become a householder and beget good progeny. Also give, give and give (*śraddhayā deyam,* etc.).' Truthfulness means straightforwardness in thought, word and deed. It means to think noble, relevant thoughts only, to express them when necessary in a precise language, and act in harmony with one's thoughts. Thus the speech of the truthful has the strength of his whole personality behind it. Therefore it cannot fail to produce its results. Truthfulness results in fulfilment without fail, says the Yoga-sūtra.[6] In fact, in realising the highest knowledge, truthfulness occupies the highest place. 'He that speaks truth always is sitting on the lap of God, as it were,' says Sri Ramakrishna. The speech of a truthful person unfailingly produces its effect, i.e., it impresses its purport on the heart of the hearer, brings succour to his distressed mind through an uttered benediction, brings fearlessness to the speaker himself! More truths are revealed sponteneously to such a truthful man. Thus truthfulness is a great value in education.

From truthfulness come honesty, punctuality, cleanliness, orderliness, simplicity, etc. Truthfulness is the guard against all duplicity, cunningness and hypocrisy. It saves the student from many a false step. It makes him work hard to get sound knowledge rather than putting up an appearance of it! It gives him an inner urge to confess his failures to the teacher and thus get corrected. A true

6. सत्यप्रतिष्ठायां क्रियाफलाश्रयत्वम् ।—*Y.S.*, 2.36

student will be humble to accept and apologize when he is in the wrong. This great quality attracts the love and solicitation from the teacher.

Tapas

We also give an important place for austerity (*tapas* in Sanskrit) in education. 'Know Brahman through tapas,' says the *Taittirīya Upaniṣad.* The practice of truthfulness, as discussed earlier, is itself a great austerity. *Satyam tapaḥ,* says the *Mahānārāyaṇa Upaniṣad.* Indeed it is so! Sri Ramakrishna, the perfect Avatāra, also says, 'Truthfulness is the austerity for the Kaliyuga (the present age).'

What is austerity and its purpose? Austerity, called tapas, literally means 'burning' or 'melting by heating.' The mind of a student has to be ridden of lethargy, lust, distracting thoughts, and spurious whims and fancies, and when this is done, the mind, like a molten metal, can take the mould of the teacher. It can assimilate the real purport of the words of the teacher. The student remains receptive to the teachings of the Guru. The student's mind takes, as it were, the shape of the Guru's enlightened mind. Sri Ramakrishna used to sing a song in Bengali, 'Mother, I will cast you into the mould of my mind and will take out your Image from it.'

Training the body to be strong and efficient, early to bed and early to rise, thus controlling sleep to minimum, practising simplicity in clothing and bedding, moderateness in eating and drinking, forbearing calmly when one is ill or punished for one's wrong—all these practised as a necessary part of education will constitute tapas and will help make the student efficient and strong.

A Taste for Excercises

Sublimation of lower impulses takes place through cultivating higher tastes like reading noble literature, singing devotional music, creating edifying art forms, healthy and hard excercises like gymnastics, games and sports, long trekking, swimming, running, and so on. A taste for training the body should be cultivated even from boyhood.

Pure Love

Love is a value which every youth is fascinated with but almost all mistake it for lust, which is selfish and jealous and results in misery. Educators should put the youth to serve the poor, the afflicted, and the needy. Then they would have a taste of what unselfish love is. Through this experience the students should be taught that any expectation of gratitude or obligation as a return should never be entertained. Love cannot be bartered for money or for favours. In love there should be no place for lust, envy, rivalry, or restrictions. It is all freedom and joy. All love relations between young people should be on a pure level like unto a father, mother, sister, brother, or a child.

Love of Music

This is another value that can sublimate the lower emotions very easily. Greek educationists advocated music as a compulsory subject in education. The writer knows the case of a college student who had a book of songs which he had learnt to sing in his student days in our school. Once when he was very depressed in his college hostel, being far away from his home, just by crooning a few songs from the book he overcame his depresion as if through a psychiatric treatment! Music can thus be a private psychotherapist attached to a student all the twenty-four hours all his life!

Prayer

Another sterling value is prayer. Vedic seers prayed and prayed in the Ṛg-vedic and Sāma-vedic hymns called Sūkta. Great saints like Jayadeva, Kabir, Surdas, Mirabai, Nanak, Chaitanya, Sri Ramakrishna and his band of apostles all would go into ecstasy through prayers. The elevating literature of prayer can teach great philosophical truths also to the young people. Prayer is not, as it is often thought, begging; it is rather reminding and demanding our paternal heritage from God who is our beloved Father and Mother in one.

There is a great universal prayer in the Vedas which should be repeated by all students—irrespective of race, gender, caste or colour. That is the Gāyatri mantra which runs thus: 'We meditate (*dhīmahi*) on the adorable spiritual effulgence (*vareṇyan bhargaḥ*) of the Divine Creator (*savituḥ*) who projects the three worlds—the gross, subtle and the causal (represented by *bhuḥ, bhuvaḥ, svaḥ*). May He enlighten our intellect.'[7] The individual intelligence imbibes the cosmic intelligence through such a prayer when practised regularly. Practice means chanting at regular intervals—at least at morning and evening hours, simultaneously meditating on its meaning. Indian education teaches this prayer to every student to arouse the dormant powers of understanding in him or her. In the past ten years there is a sudden interest awakened in the public in this country towards this mantra. Numerous schools, colleges, and public prayer places have regular chanting of this mantra which augurs well.

Sraddha

Śraddhā is another value whose place in education can never be over-emphasized. Śraddhā in a student is not only his faith in his teacher but it is also an indomitable will to acquire knowledge at any cost. Śraddhā is self-confidence. It is faith in the unfailing cosmic power behind one's individual self. It can face failures with smiles, and renew further efforts with fresh hopes. One with Śraddhā is ever resourceful. No obstacle is too big for him to overcome. Śraddhā is capacity to shoulder any responsibility with efficiency and sacrifice. Śraddhā is, as it were, the philosopher's stone that can convert any obstacle into a stepping stone to success.

Wisdom, the Goal

Wisdom and not mere knowledge is considered the goal of all education. Wisdom is to know what is permanent and what is not and to reject the latter. In the early stages of the student this is possible only by emulating the ideal characters in the milieu in which the student finds himself.

---

7. ॐ भूर्भुवस्वः तत्सवितुर्वरेण्यं भर्गो देवस्य धीमहि । धियो यो नः प्रचोदयात् ॥

For example, in the Indian context contemplating on the lives of Rama, Krishna, Buddha, Christ, Nanak, Chaitanya, Ramakrishna, and Vivekananda can help in cultivating this wisdom. A reverence to all religious leaders cultivated during student life can narrow down the gap between the various socio-religious communities in this country. Religious harmony is a sweet fruit of the tree of wisdom. I recall here an experience.

At Along, in the state of Arunachal Pradesh, the tribal boys pray in our hostels daily before the pictures of several prophets, all of equal size and decorated on an altar. The pictures are of Sri Ramakrishna, Holy Mother, Swami Vivekananda, Jesus, Buddha, Nanak, and Zoroaster. It has been observed that, after a few years in our school, our students feel and say, 'We belong to all religions because we are from the Ramakrishna Mission.' The point to note here is that they are not taught any 'harmony of religions'! This liberal attitude is one great value that our education has to inculcate in all students of our country to strengthen its social and religious fabric.

Conclusion

Religion has to be explained to our students as the growth in character, the virtues of which are self-control, selfless service, practice of prayer, to love all people and to help them in need. These form the real core of every religion. All religious heads should come together to prepare a 'book of common religious teachings'—those that help cultivate the above values without contradicting anything in any religion. This can be taught with profit to engender a brotherly love between all religious groups which is the need of the hour. To the extent we can instil dharma into all our students, to that extent we will surely succeed in stemming the rot we see around our country. Macaulay wanted to de-Hinduize this country in 1836; strangely, in the same year Sri Ramakrishna was born and he rebelled against Macaulay's system. He refused to go for book-learning. He would rather go in for the old Vedic system of education by hearing, chanting, memorizing, contemplating, serving and self-sacrificing. He matured into the finest flower of spirituality, the greatest one after the great incarnation, Sri Krishna of *Mahābhārata.* Sri Ramakrishna's influence on the world has been recognized by great savants like Max Müller, Romain Rolland and great historians like Dr. Arnold Toynbee. Vivekananda and Gandhi, following the spiritual traditions of Indian education, flowered into the greatest leaders of this nation. In contrast, a statistical study of the three generations after our national Independence who have received the Macaulayan education can be studied. Each succeeding generation will be observed plummetting lower and lower to its predecesor in morals and patriotic fervour! Referring to the amoral way of educating the people at that time, which has come down right to our present time, Sister Nivedita wrote: 'To close against any gates of the higher life is a sin far greater than murder, for, it means responsibility for spiritual death, for inner bondage, and the result is ruin unspeakable.'

The values in education alone can save us from the 'ruin unspeakable' the Sister has spoken of and with which we started this essay.

9
Values for School Children

PIERRETTE MOHAN

We all think we have a clear idea of what education is and which values we should develop in our children. It is quite easy really. We try to instil in them the values which we ourselves cherish. The difficulty arises when they reach their teens and ask us, 'Why did you educate me in such a stupid way?' We then remember that it is the same question we had asked our parents when we were of the same age. We also remember that we had always thought: 'Me, I'll manage better'!

When you are—as it is in my case—working in an educational system, things are slightly different. You cannot choose the values, just as you cannot choose the subjects or the schedules. They are already in place and you have to accept them. It is of no use to dream of changing them completely, but if you examine them with attention, you will see that there is always an opportunity to modify them more or less in your own way so that they will become adjusted with what you are and what you would like to practise with the students.

In fact, the schools where I worked, and still work as a counsellor, are quite good. These are the kind of schools where the children are tough and that makes the educational team, from the sweeper to the Principal, come rather close to one another in order to face the students, understand their problems, and find a way to help them. Certainly the students have points that could be better, certainly a few people do not care for anything or anybody except themselves. But this you'll find everywhere.

You see, the important point is that we have to try to make children who are so different in culture, colour, religion, social background, etc., enter inside the same frame of values and knowledge. And when they are inside that frame and they have assimilated it, we must bring them to a point, different for each one, a point where they will have started to discover and to develop what is hidden in their inner self, a point where, if we want, with just a small push we can send them in their own orbits of life, a bit like when we cultivate rosebuds we hope they will transform themselves into roses, all different, but all beautiful in their own way. That is why, I think, schools exist to grow different but beautiful flowers in the hearts of the growing generation.

Nowadays knowledge has become so wide and so evolving that we cannot hope to teach a lot to a child. What we say today will be obsolete tomorrow and the child *is* tomorrow. So, more than knowledge, what we have to develop in the child is the *taste* for knowledge, the curiosity that is dormant in the young mind, and which has to be awakened in the same way as an ox pulling a cart is forced to advance with a whip. The 'whip' for the child is the will that we put in his or her hands, the will that transforms all, the will that, with God's grace, allows us to handle our own life, the will that would help manifest the potential power and talents of the child.

In our schools in France, the frame is based on our favourite French values and we feel that if we manage to instil them into the maximum number of brains, all other values will automatically follow.

Our first value is undenominationalism. We can give many definitions for it. The most usual is: 'Undenominationalism is that which rejects any idea of religion.' I would prefer to say: '...that which *accepts* any idea of religion.' Once this positive notion is put on the table, we can start to work with the young minds and make them slowly glide from the thought 'My religion is the best' to the idea 'My religion is good and other religions are good too.' That is the beginning of questioning, the beginning of the quest that will finish always at the same point, the essential, the One who is in our heart. Because of this, you see, I like undenominationalism and I stand up for it.

I also like freedom, and I support and defend that too. Because, as you know, even if we are a part of a family or of a society, every one of us is unique. We have to be our own masters. Freedom, however, needs a long apprenticeship, and the child will have to be helped in that study. First, a boy will have to know himself, to search out who he really is. Then he will learn how to analyse, to discriminate, to synthesize and, finally, to decide calmly, without passion, controlling his instincts and impulses, what is best and in harmony with his inner self. Who else can know all this better than him?

The next value is equality. I like equality and I fight for it. Do you know why? Society is based on differences and that is all right. What is *not* all right is when the difference is counted in terms of worth. I am here in the social scale or I know this and you do not, so I have more, or less, worth than you—all this is nonsense. The school must be a place where everybody is treated in the same way, doing what is necessary to put all the children at the level where they should be. For instance, the school must give free teaching to all, free tuitions to complete the lessons if necessary (some children need just a bit more time to understand things), scholarships to the needy families so that a child who is able and wishes to study will have the opportunity to do it as long as necessary, keeping his or her dignity, thinking 'I am in school/college/university because I deserve to be here and not because my parents have money to maintain me' or '...because I have the advantage of entering in the reserved quota.' In this way the child will know what equality is and will practise it.

Equality induces another value—and that is solidarity. And—you have guessed it!—I like solidarity and I stand up for it. We are all in the same current of universal life, receiving tons of gifts and blessings from it and we have to keep the balance; whatever we have received, we must return to universal life in some form or other. We can do that in many ways. Love is not the easiest way. It has to be practised intensively and correctly. With the help of teachers and counsellors, the child will learn not only to love friends, which is quite easy, but also to love others in the same way, to love even that little rascal who has just stolen one's favourite pen. That will bring our children real peace and happiness. 'Since wars begin in the minds of men, it is in the minds of men that the defences of peace must be constructed,' says the preamble to the charter of UNESCO.

Social work is also a good way to obey the law of sacrifice. Social work is not possible without love, love for others and also love for one's true self. To organize social activities is an important duty of any school. The child should feel that he or she is unique and is also, at the same time, a part of society. Here I would like to quote a sentence of Swami Vivekananda: 'What would be this kind of liberation where you leave behind your people lost in ignorance and unhappiness?'

As I reach my conclusion, I will finish with what we often say to our students here: 'Do well in your own way whatever has to be done, try to do it with enthusiasm, but without any attachment and always with the idea that it should make you and your fellows progress on the *right* way.'

10
Values in Administration

D. K. OZA

I have been shouldering administrative responsibilities since the last forty years. Throughout this period I have tried to observe the events in India, its public life, its politics, and its administration. What I now write is partly determined by my training, partly by temperament, and partly by experience. All of us form our opinions and pass judgments by combining these three elements, don't we?

I must begin with a short autobiographical note. Throughout my school and college years there was not even a single day of strike or violence by students. Our examinations were held on schedule and valuation was strict. (If a student got 75% marks, he or she would probably top the list among 10,000 students; nowadays student-evaluation is so liberal that getting 95% marks is not unusual.) Sports were encouraged. Girls in our class were treated with respect. We also respected our teachers, who sometimes commanded even awe and fear. A few teachers were extremely friendly, but even then we took no stupid liberties with them. Not a single teacher absented himself from work, unless he was ill.

In those days there were not many caste distinctions in the student community. It is, of course, true that some students were snobbish, but most students chose their friends from like-minded people irrespective of caste. Of my four best friends in college, one was a Jew, one was a Christian, and two were Hindus. These days some students form their friendship on the basis of caste and sub-caste, thanks to various 'progressive laws' enacted by State and Central Governments who are very keen to ensure 'social justice' through inciting caste hatreds.

I discovered Swami Vivekananda through booklets in Gujarati, my mother tongue. No one who reads him even once can remain untouched by what he said. In mid-1940s, when I was about twelve, I started reading Gandhian literature. I found it fascinating. I could read English only when I was about eighteen and so my discovery of Nehru had to wait till the early 1950s. I am a very avid reader, and if I once get interested in a book I generally try to finish it in a single sitting. By the time I was twenty-one I could read English well. I learnt Hindi without any formal classes.

When I joined the Indian Administrative Service training in 1957 for a year, the occasional visitors who spoke to us were men and women of great distinction.

I particularly remember Swami Ranganathananda, who gave us three lectures, and Sri Pyarelal and Sri Kalelkar, both of whom were Gandhians. After a great deal of reading and thinking and seeing life, I have come to the conclusion that if we combine the philosophy of Swami Vivekananda and Mahatma Gandhi, India can be fully regenerated. Most of our politicians—I am sorry to say—are ignorant and stupid men. I do not think many of them have read these two pathfinders, but we should never give up the hope of making our politicians literate.

My thinking regarding values in administration is conditioned by my upbringing and training, as described above. I shall now state my points briefly.

First, administration must be transparent. Nothing should be done in secret. Secrecy breeds evil. The reasons for taking a decision must be recorded for all to see. This will also help to eliminate the almost universal corruption in politics and administration today.

Second, decisions must be taken in the public interest. This phrase, 'public interest,' must be understood properly. No decision should be taken under any kind of pressure. Every decision should be such as benefits the whole community. The decision must be able to stand close scrutiny. This was the first lesson we learnt from those who trained us in the Civil Service in the early years. I think nowadays this is totally ignored.

What do I mean by taking decision without being pressured? For example, if some Christians make a reasonable request for a piece of land to be used as a burial ground, the decision should not be influenced by communalist propaganda of anti-Christian fanatics. If the Hindus request that some grant should be made for propagation of the Sanskrit language, it should not be turned down on the ground of secularism. The same would apply if the Muslims made a request for assistance to promote the Urdu language.

Third, civil servants should leave behind their caste, community, religion, and language in their own homes. They should not carry these labels with them when they go to work. At the workplace a civil servant is just a public servant acting in the public interest, trying to serve the public.

Fourth, corruption must be ruthlessly punished, regardless of whether the culprit is a politician or a government official. Corruption has now gone so deep that it is very difficult to implement this suggestion. Even minor acts of corruption must be mercilessly exposed. The Gandhian method is to boycott a politician or official who is suspected of dishonesty. Where there is reasonable proof of dishonesty, that person must be thrown out of public life, and should be sent to jail and asked to do hard labour for three years, and so on. All this is very important.

Fifth, special privileges should not be given to politicians and officials. They should not be allowed to live in luxury at public expense, they should not be permitted to absent themselves from duty on flimsy pretexts such as 'public holidays,' they should reach office on time and should work hard. Once I suggested to the Government of India that since Mahatma Gandhi worked almost twenty-four hours a day, his birthday, 2nd of October, should be celebrated by working two hours extra on that day instead of declaring it as a holiday. To this I received a reply that

15th August, 26th January, and 2nd October are national holidays. I am still keeping the letter with me.

Sixth, persons at all levels in the government must be encouraged to think and to give their advice freely. The superior officer or the minister should not assume that he has the key to all wisdom.

Seventh, by far the most important thing about India is the poverty of its masses. The entire administration must be geared to tackle this problem. In order to achieve this, all government staff and politicians must be given one book of hundred pages, half of it devoted to the teachings of Swami Vivekananda, and the remaining half to the teachings of Mahatma Gandhi. I am specifically referring to the teachings where these two men spoke about the poor, the oppressed, the dispossessed, the helpless. Every government officer should be asked to pass an oral test on this book.

There must be, moreover, a continuing evaluation of every one in the government. One Christian organization calls this 'ongoing clarification of thought.'

Eighth, voluntary organizations and nongovernmental agencies must be encouraged, because they are more capable of serving the people and of mobilizing the poor. In many cases the administration must take its guidelines from such voluntary, public-spirited groups.

These values in administration can be enforced only if the Indian public is vigilant and the newspapers are aggressive in their approach to the tyrannies and failures of our decision-makers.

11

The Values of Law and the Law of Values

CHARLES KINGMAN MITCHELL

Lawyers (I confess I am one of them) are supposed to be governed by a code of conduct called *legal ethics,* a term often compared to such oxymorons as *military intelligence* and *political wisdom.* Indeed, the code of legal ethics is open to varying interpretations, most of which permit a great deal of questionable behaviour. But this does not distinguish it from any other set of rules by which human conduct is supposed to be governed. Like all such rules, legal ethics are often more honoured in the breach than in the observance.

Conduct is governed by values insofar as it is governed at all. The Code of Legal Ethics, like law itself, is a package of values reduced to writing, codified, and imposed upon people by the coercive power of government. But mostly, values are not so much what is written in statutes, or even what we think consciously, as they are what we have internalized in the process of living. My parents taught me certain values, some by what they said, more by what they did. Some of the early values that still remain with me are those I learned through association. I grew up with a bunch of hard-playing, hard-fighting, mischievous, fiercely loyal country boys. To this day I find within myself such principles as, 'Stand up for your friends, no matter what it costs you,' 'Play to win,' 'Never snitch.'

In addition to teachings, example by conduct, and associations, I also internalized values through what I can only call 'inspiration'. It came most powerfully via a combination of great teachings and great living: Buddha, Christ, Ramakrishna, for example, or Lincoln and Gandhi in the sphere of politics. Inspired values also came to me from great thought expressed through great art, as in Whitman, Wordsworth, Emerson, Thoreau. These inspirational figures had in common an inner law that completely governed their behaviour without regard to, and often in derogation of, the laws and values of their time.

Law imposes the values of some segment of the population upon all the rest of the population. In a democracy it is one form of the 'tyranny of the majority' or, all too often, the tyranny of an economically or politically powerful minority. This is why Emerson said in *Self-Reliance,* 'Good men must not obey the laws too well,' why Jesus drove the money changers from the temple. Law is often corrupt, and it is always weak just insofar as its values are imposed from without rather than grown from within by teachings, the conduct of others, associations or inspiration. If the values of the law are not my values, I will break the law, and so will many people much of the time, all people some of the time, and some people all of the time.

Unfortunately, at the present stage of its development humanity is incapable of achieving order without law. One group's idea of order is another's idea of oppression, and so prisons brim with people who are legally 'criminals' but who have done no external harm. Prostitutes and their customers. Drug users. Political prisoners:

> Oh, Paddy dear, an' did ye hear the news that's goin' round?
> The shamrock is by law forbid to grow on Irish ground!
> No more St. Patrick's Day we'll keep; his colour can't be seen.
> For there's a cruel new law agin' the wearin' o' the green.[1]

Nevertheless, although this is the law at its worst, law is the servant of order, and order in society is the root value beneath all civil and criminal law. The fact that laws are often stupid and counterproductive is merely the logical result of the fact that they are enacted by creatures who are so primitive they cannot otherwise govern themselves.

At its best, the law is the servant of inspired values, but to get it into such a high-functioning state is an uphill crawl. The practice of law (among honest lawyers, and there are such things) is a constant struggle to make the rules of law function as instruments of justice. In this effort the

1. In 1794 British Parliamentary reform stalled and the Catholics of Ireland were again denied seats. In protest, they wore shamrocks, a three-leafed clover said to have been adopted by St. Patrick as the symbol of the Trinity. Fearing rebellion, Parliament banned the wearing of shamrocks. This anonymous song appeared c. 1795.

values of law often collide with such inspired values as *truth* or *truthfulness,* a value that has particular power for me both because I drank it in from Christ and Ramakrishna and also because it was stressed in my parents' house from my earliest memories. Yet famed defence lawyer, Harvard University law professor and author, Alan M. Dershowitz observed in an interview in *U.S. News and World Report* (August 9, 1982):

> All sides in a trial want to hide at least some of the truth. The defendant wants to hide the truth because he's generally guilty. The defence attorney's job is to make sure the jury does not arrive at that truth. The prosecution, too, has a truth to hide: it wants to make sure the process by which the evidence was obtained is not truthfully presented because, as often as not, that process will raise questions.

I have been in this position. My client, Mr. Right, worked for BAD-X Co. for 25 years. He was good at his job, loyal, diligent, regularly promoted. Then, when he turned 50 years old, BAD-X Co. fired him. The ostensible reason was that he was slipping BAD-X Co. trade secrets to a woman at Rival Company.

He wasn't and BAD-X knows he wasn't. It's a lie. I can prove it. I can prove that Rival Company got its data from perfectly legal reverse engineering. BAD-X Co. wanted to get rid of Mr. Right because they did not want to incur the burden of his retirement, his pension was about to vest, he was earning more than they wanted to pay, he was too old, he had a bad back and they were afraid he would injure it and incur paid downtime. They also had made a high-level decision to replace all workers over 50 with much younger ones—at half the pay. I have subpoenaed all of BAD-X's corporate records, its internal memoranda, notes from management meetings. I can prove all of this.

Ah, but Mr. Right *was* in fact having an extramarital affair with the lady from Rival Company. If BAD-X discovers it, my client's case is lost no matter how many lies BAD-X has told, no matter how brutal and wrong they have been. I must keep this truth away from the jury. It is my job, my solemn *duty* as part of my profession, to keep the truth out of court. The Code of Legal Ethics permits it. So do my boyhood values: Stand up for your friends no matter what it costs you; play hard; never snitch.

Do I do it? Do I try every ploy I can think of to cover up Mr. Right's affair? Indeed I do. The affair is irrelevant. *Yes,* he had the affair, and *Yes,* he's a cheat and a liar in that context, but he did *not* steal the trade secrets, and BAD-X never thought he did—the whole thing is a mere pretext, part of BAD-X's secret game plan to get rid of older employees, a game plan that is blatantly illegal, not to mention brutal, immoral and unfair.

On the other hand, what about my commitment to truthfulness? Well, I will not lie to win Mr. Right's case, but that somewhat begs the question. I am, after all, in the circumstances set forth here, doing my best to prevent the truth from getting into court. The question is insoluble unless I make the end, justice, justify the means—a risky proposition at best. But I must do what my feelings tell me is right. I must rely, or try to rely, not on the Code of Ethics but on the same inner law that guided all the great teachers of inspired values down through history.

The reality of extrinsic law is that it is a weak bastion of values. The reality of values is that they are weak governors of conduct unless they are the kind of inner law obeyed by Gandhi and Thoreau, Christ and Ramakrishna. Emerson believed that there exists a transcendental entity, a spirit, which is a living Moral Law in the hearts of human beings. Everybody has it, he believed, and we can hear its counsel if we will only listen.

I believe it, too, although not precisely in Emerson's terms. Once in a while I even see it in the practice of law, feeble font of values that it is. It happens, for instance, when people who have lied outside of court swear in court to tell the truth and then, to their own surprise, tell it, overwhelmed by that pure inner spirit. But for the most part we primitive little humans will make and break our extrinsic laws until we have evolved to the point where we can hear and obey the intrinsic law that rarely, rarely finds its way to court.

12

Time for National Introspection

NANI A. PALKHIVALA

World history moves in cycles. High ethical times are succeeded by low, decadent decades. Today we in India are at the nadir of moral values. The size of the crime wave and armed violence, which is so huge as to baffle criminologists, is symptomatic of our ethical degradation.

A commercial recession can be quickly transformed into a buoyant economy; but a moral recession cannot be shaken off for years. The rot in public life began after the death of Lal Bahadur Shastri and has been increasing at a galloping rate. It has spread so far as to contaminate the higher judiciary which is the soul of any democracy. Judges are the noblest servants of society: without them, its most fundamental equilibriums cannot be maintained.

The poisoning of the well-spring of justice began in 1973 when the three seniormost judges of the Supreme Court, who were independent enough to decide against the executive in *Kesavananda*'s case, were superseded upon the Chief Justice's office falling vacant. The government expressly proclaimed that it wanted 'committed' judges—committed to the ideology of the ruling party. That began an era of a judiciary made to measure. The government looked out for pliant judges who had no more backbone than a chocolate éclair.

Evil is more infectious than AIDS and, if unchecked, progresses with an inevitable momentum of its own. It is but one step from forsaking intellectual integrity to forsaking financial integrity. A judge who decides wrongly out of motives of self-promotion is no less corrupt than a judge who decides wrongly out of motives of financial gain.

The slide on the inclined plane has been rapid and unmistakable. In the first two decades of our republic it was the compulsion of veracity, not the fear of the law relating to contempt of court, which was responsible for the fact that no charges of corruption were levelled against the judiciary. Now the compulsion of veracity dictates such charges, in defiance of the Contempt of Courts Act.

It is preeminently a time for deep, national introspection. We must bury our self-esteem fifty fathoms deep, and be self-critical enough to meet the truth face to face. The Bar is more commercialized than ever before. It is against all change, specially change for the better. Today the law is looked upon, not as a *learned* profession but as a *lucrative* one. The due process of law has become less 'due' than tortuous and unending.

If you lose faith in politicians, you can change them. If you lose faith in judges, you still have to live with them. The ineluctable fact is that the conduct of some judicial officers in different courts has been far from exemplary in terms of ethics.

Corruption in the upper reaches of the judiciary is illustrative of the incredible debasement of our national character. There is general public acceptance of venality everywhere as a venial idiosyncrasy. We are merely amused by the fact that the contrast between the moral tone of ancient India and that of modern India is sufficient to disprove the theory of evolution upwards!

The question is—which is the best way of dealing with a corrupt judge in the higher courts without creating a crisis of public faith in the judiciary?

The greatest illusion of our people is their infantile belief in the legal solubility of all problems. In the wise words of Lord Hailsham, the former Lord Chancellor of the UK, 'We might do well to remember that in the whole realm of human relations there is no field more vulnerable to corruption, dishonesty, chicanery, and sheer quackery and charlatanism than contested litigation, criminal and civil, commercial, matrimonial, testamentary, or resulting from personal injury, real, imagined, or invented. We might also do well to consider that few of the safeguards we have achieved against these evils have been achieved by government interference or by parliamentary legislation. They have been brought about by the steady application of self-regulatory procedures and disciplines ...'

Impeachment proceedings in Parliament—the only constitutional way of removing a judge of a High Court or the Supreme Court from his office—is a procedure not to be resorted to lightly. It is enormously cumbersome and is likely to bring political passions into play. A striking example of the malfunctioning of our democracy is afforded by the fact that the first impeachment proceeding ever sought to be started in our Parliament was that against one of our finest judges, J. C. Shah, a judge of impeccable integrity. It was a move commenced by a disgruntled, dishonest civil servant against whom Justice Shah had given a judgment in the Supreme Court, and who cunningly managed to secure as many as 199 signatures of Members of Parliament for an appeal to the Speaker of the Lok Sabha to start impeachment proceedings against the judge. In 1993, a motion to impeach Justice V. Ramaswamy of the Supreme Court was defeated in Parliament because the Congress party issued a whip that Congress members should abstain from voting, ignoring the correct legal position that Parliament had to exercise a quasi-judicial function on an impeachment motion.

It would be foolish as well as dangerous to relax the rigour of the Contempt of Courts Act, 1971 and permit truth to be pleaded as a defence when an allegation of corruption is made against a judge. Character assassination is the national sport of India, and some dissatisfied litigants and lawyers will have no hesitation in making allegations which would scandalize the court and then inviting the judge to face a public inquiry for a length of time which would make eternity intelligible.

In the past there have been sufficient instances of the executive interfering in matters pertaining to the judiciary for ulterior, ill-founded reasons, to dissuade an honest law minister from establishing another precedent of intermeddling even for well-founded reasons.

Perhaps the best way of dealing with the problem is to have a law, or even an unwritten convention, regarding the procedure to be followed when there are allegations of corruption against any judge. The matter should be placed confidentially before the Chief Justice of the High Court for inquiring into the case. If his view is that there is no substance in the allegations, the matter should be regarded as closed. If he thinks otherwise, the case should be referred to the Chief Justice of India and two Supreme Court judges. If the decision of the three judges (which would be final) is adverse, the errant judge may well regard discretion as the better part of valour and decide not to continue on the Bench. This would be a dignified and quietly effective way of dealing with men unworthy of holding high judicial office.

Luckily, the overwhelming majority of our judges in the eighteen High Courts and the Supreme Court are men of integrity, while some of them combine character with outstanding calibre.

13
Values in the Police Force

JULIO RIBEIRO

The primary duty of the police is to protect the life and property of the citizens. The police have also to keep order on the streets and regulate traffic to ensure that economic and social activities move at the required pace. Hence their role is tied up with a lot of responsibility. Even an ordinary policeman, who is not particularly well-educated or well-paid, has the power to arrest and detain other citizens, some of whom may be economically, socially and educationally his superiors.

This is a tremendous power given to the police. In the hands of small and unscrupulous men, people without a sense of values, the power can be grossly misused. Nevertheless, every State needs a police force to maintain law and order in its territory. Without a police force the State can sink into chaos and confusion.

The extent of misuse of police powers varies from country to country. It varies according to the different values and cultures existing in those countries. It was widely acknowledged, for example, that the English and the Japanese police were service-oriented, and accepted by their people as friends. Ordinary citizens were quite happy to approach the English 'Bobby' on the streets for directions or the Japanese policeman in his 'Koban' for advice. Even in these countries the situation has now changed. For socio-economic and demographic reasons, the old equations no longer hold true. The English and the Japanese police will reflect the changes in their respective societies just as our police in India reflect society as it presently exists and will change if the attitudes and values of our society change.

In India, as in the United States—or in most other countries of the world—the police are trained to be law-enforcers. This is because external sanctions play a more important part than internal sanctions to prevent breaches of law. In our country, for example, perfectly respectable citizens have no compunction in breaching traffic laws or violating financial regulations enshrined in the Income Tax, Sales Tax or other fiscal statutes. This conscious or subconscious breach of laws, considered to be unfair, breeds a contempt for law at all levels.

When the higher strata of society, represented by the haves, commit white-collar crimes like the evasion of taxes, and then proceed to flaunt their wealth at family weddings or children's birthday parties, the have-nots in turn are tempted to make easy money by breaking other laws. They cannot commit white-collar crimes because they are not educated or affluent enough to avoid Income Tax, Sales Tax or Wealth Tax. Nor are they in a position to amass wealth through bribery, fraud, forgery, or cheating. This type of crime is the prerogative of those affluent members of society who possess a yen for getting rich at any cost.

The middle class citizens are more bothered about the bank robber who uses knife and gun than those of their own class who forge or cheat. They conveniently forget that the example has been set by members of their own class who, by their indecent show of wealth, have tempted the have-nots to use illegal means to acquire money.

The policeman in India is drawn from the ranks of the have-nots. He will naturally mirror the attitudes and the culture and the prejudices of the have-nots. His officers, who come mainly from the middle class, will reflect the values and culture of that class. This is a fact of life which cannot be wished away.

The middle classes in any society are supposed to be the backbone of the moral conscience of the people. When the middle classes themselves succumb to the temptations of consumerism, materialism and the get-rich-quick-by-any-means syndrome, then this newly-acquired culture is bound to be reflected in the police hierarchy as well. Simultaneously, the police at the lower ranks will try and emulate their betters.

In today's India, every policeman yearns for a television, a motor-cycle or a scooter, electronic gadgets and other such possessions that denote rising expectations and the 'good life.' Since he cannot get it in the legitimate manner within his salary, he does so through corruption, a phenomenon that has affected his seniors also.

In the past, senior offers used to provide examples of rectitude and good behaviour. The juniors could not cite them as excuses for their own sins. The position is quite different today, where the distinction between seniors and juniors in the realm of values and proper behaviour has been obliterated.

Police officers and men in any country of the world are drawn from the same society that they are called upon to police. Inevitably, they will reflect the attitudes and values of the society from which they are drawn. If society is violent, the police will be violent. If society is corrupt, the police will be corrupt. It is difficult, almost impossible, to expect policemen to be like oasis in a desert when all around they are surrounded by perfidy and vice. It is ridiculous to expect policemen to possess qualities superior to the rest of their fellow citizens.

The ideal policeman is one who is humane, honest, intelligent, helpful, polite, sensitive to human suffering and human wants, both physical and emotional. The ideal policeman is one who takes prompt and effective action according to the laws of the land. The ideal policeman should be respected and admired by law-abiding citizens. He should be feared only by law-breakers.

Unfortunately, the image of a policeman in India is exactly the opposite. He is seen as boorish, insensitive, corrupt, and inhuman. He is seen as a friend of criminals. He is avoided by the law-abiding, who hesitate to approach him for help even in dire circumstances.

This public concept of the average policeman is unfortunately justified. As values in Indian society decline, as unbridled consumerism envelopes not only the cities but also the smaller towns of India, penetrating sometimes to its villages with the advent of television, particularly cable television, the urge to acquire consumer goods touches all spheres of human and economic endeavour. Values have deteriorated in every segment of society, even in the noble professions like medicine and teaching. It is unrealistic to expect that this same deterioration would not be reflected in the police force.

The same middle classes that have fallen a prey to modern values, ironically, expect police officers and men to possess all the good qualities that they themselves are discarding. For example, loud-mouthed businessmen who have no scruples about the methods they employ to make money, talk very glibly in their drawing rooms and at club meetings about police corruption. They themselves indulge in all the known vices and yet expect the much lower paid and less educated policemen to be better human beings than they are.

This is not to condone police transgressions. This is an attempt to explain the general fall in values in every sphere of societal activity and to show how it has had its inevitable fallout in the value system of the police. I do believe, however, that policemen should be better behaved and more dignified than even those who are their betters in terms of economic, social and educational status. This is because the police have a vital duty to perform, the duty to protect the life and property of the citizens.

This is an onerous duty, requiring a higher value system and genuine concern for the poor and the defenceless. Careful selection of new recruits and inculcation of moral and spiritual values during training to change the mindsets of the new entrants will help. It is gratifying that police training colleges across the country have now already started trying to do this. Unfortunately, many idealistic young men lose their idealism when they finish training and begin their careers in the field.

I made an attempt to remind them of their responsibilities in the Police Commissionerate of Thane, in the early 1980s. About 70 officers and men, including one Deputy Commissioner/Assistant Commissioner, 3 Inspectors, 7 Sub-Inspectors, 15 Head Constables and 45 Constables, at a time, were asked to undergo a two-week 'Changing the Mindset' course at police headquarters. This captive audience was exposed to talks based on their own personal experiences and intellectual perceptions by ordinary citizens including students, workers in factories, managers, women, doctors, lawyers, retired policemen and others. Mother Teresa, and a Jain Muni visiting from the United States, also participated in the exercise. One leading woman-writer in Marathi, Shantabai Shelke, wrote later about her interaction with these policemen. She said that she once went to buy flowers in a shop and she was surprised to find an ordinary policeman in uniform also buying flowers there. She said that she never expected a policeman to have that soft touch associated with flowers. She was reflecting the general view of policemen and it was very satisfying for me to realise that my invitation to this famous writer had changed her own view about the police.

But coming back to the experiment. The officers and men were so affected by what they heard and discussed with their interlocutors that they were enthused to take strong and effective action against all antisocial activities like bootlegging, gambling and extortions. The effect of their conversion was so electrifying that the people of the Commissionerate of Thane acknowledged that for once they could breathe freely after years of abandoning any hope of doing so. When I was transferred to Bombay, twenty policemen insisted on speaking at the farewell function. Normally only one officer speaks a few platitudes on behalf of the assembled officers and men. Here the policemen themselves insisted on speaking and each of them mentioned about the effect of the course on their attitudes and how they had regained their self-respect. One policeman, who was addicted to heavy drinking and whose problem was discussed in the course, stood up to say that he had now kicked the habit. His fellow policemen clapped.

It is essential in any such training programmes to devalue material and selfish interests and to stress on self-esteem and satisfaction in work done well. It should also be stressed that the policeman is best placed in any society to do good to the people at large, particularly to the poor and the needy.

The best policeman is he who is a good social worker, ready to help women in distress, street children, those forced into prostitution, and others similarly doomed by fate. If the police can spread the message of compassion and concern for their fellowmen, that would raise them to a level where they can be the purveyors of new values in a world sinking into crass materialism.

14

The Power of Music

PRAVRAJIKA VARADAPRANA

Music, more than any other art form, has the power to affect our moods, for better or worse. It can concentrate, soothe, invigorate, and uplift the mind. Or conversely, it can agitate, scatter, or dull the mind.

Music can be an important tool for both happiness and spiritual growth if discrimination is used in the choice of music we hear. I'm speaking from the perspective of Western classical music, since that is my area of knowledge.

In Europe most of the early music was written for the church, inspired by the Bible and the life of Jesus. The Gregorian and Ambrosian chants of unearthly purity were sung in churches, convents and monasteries, echoing the spirituality of the time. Chants of the Orthodox churches

(Russian, Greek and Syrian) have a more florid, exotic flavour and are equally beautiful. These timeless chants are still sung and appreciated today.

Some of the most exquisite choral music was written during the Renaissance period in Europe. One is captivated by the purity of style and the beauty of harmonies in the motets and madrigals of that period.

Much of the music of Johann Sebastian Bach was written for performance in the churches where he was organist and music director. The magnificence of his music—his unique harmonies and intricate counterpoint—have never been surpassed. The deeply-moving quality of his music has made him one of the world's most popular composers.

The influence of religion on music gradually lessened, and some of the purity and innocence of the early music was lost. However, in every century there have been composers of great genius.

Music expresses the gamut of human and divine emotions. The most sublime music uplifts and soothes the mind, bringing joy to the listener. This type of music may be serene, noble, soaring, or powerful. Some music is so ethereal one feels it borders on the divine.

The composer needs to follow his or her highest instincts in order to create music that is uplifting and healing. There is some music on the market today which appeals to the baser instincts, with lyrics sometimes expressing the rage and frustration of the ghetto and disadvantaged. Music can certainly be light and even whimsical without losing its moral integrity.

Because so much music has already been written, it becomes increasingly difficult for the composer to be both original and inspirational. Some modern composers, in their desire to be innovative or to express the chaos and discord of our times, have lost the inspiration that can uplift humankind. To portray the world as it is may be honest, but is it constructive?

Although simple music can be trite and unimaginative, great music can be perfectly simple as exemplified in the music of Gabriel Faure. In his Requiem Mass, he combined serenely simple melodies with harmonies so subtle and moving that it touches the heart.

While the composer has the creative freedom to write music according to his or her own light, the listener also has the freedom to select music that best suits his or her tastes and value system. In the modern world it is easy for us to hear the music of our choice on the radio, tape recorder or compact disc.

For the musician, it takes many years of hard practice to perfect his or her art. This develops one-pointed concentration and discipline which can be applied to meditation. Learning to play expressively in unison with other musicians develops an awareness and sensitivity in the artist.

Fine musicians place the intentions of the composer above their own desire to shine and express themselves. Their absorption in the music allows them to rise above their own egos, thus bringing out the beauty of the music as intended by the composer. They become one with the music, as it were.

Scientists who have made studies with musicians' brains find that there is a particular area in the left side of the brain that deals with music. Musical people are born with this area of the brain already developed, but it can be further enhanced with practice.

In young children this area of the brain develops more quickly. Children who show signs of musical talent should start studying music at a young age, the younger the better. Children can acquire musical skills quickly and with a minimum of pain. Moreover, practising their art develops their concentration, and creates a habit of self-discipline at an early age.

When children do not have musical talent, there is no point in forcing them to study it. Instead, parents can give their children an opportunity to hear fine music so they can develop a taste for it, along with the current popular music that they will be exposed to.

Experiments have been made by playing different types of music while children were studying. They found that classical music, particularly the music of Mozart, enhanced the students' concentration and actually increased their IQ.

Music has successfully been used in therapy to help the physically ill, the mental ill, and severely retarded children. Autistic children who could not respond to anything else would get up and dance to music.

When one is feeling low or depressed, listening to music can help change the mood when nothing else helps. We can consider the effect of music on the mind from the standpoint of the guṇas, the three qualities that affect the moods of our minds. When we are feeling dull and lethargic (tāmasic), music of a lively, vibrant nature (rājasic) can pull us out of that mood. When we are feeling restless and agitated (rājasic) we can be calmed down by music that is serene and peaceful (sāttvic).

Music can draw the mind out into the world of māyā, or it can concentrate the mind and elevate it to a higher level of consciousness. The test of good music for the spiritual aspirant is whether or not it is compatible with the thought of God.

Why does music have such a deep effect on the psyche? Sound, related to the element space, is closest to Brahman. Swami Brahmananda, the spiritual son of Sri Ramakrishna, said that music is 'sound-Brahman.' He advised that one can approach God through music.

Religious music has a special value for the spiritual aspirant, and creates the deepest impact on the mind. There are now many American Vedantist musicians who compose songs in folk and classical idioms. Their music comes right from the heart, and touches the hearts of their listeners. Their words are usually original, or are taken from the scriptures, Bengali devotional songs, or other spiritual texts.

The art of writing vocal music is to wed the music to the words in such a way that it brings the text to life. The composers of the German lieder (songs) in the last century perfected this art. The great lieder singers also express the mood and colour of the words, bringing the song to life.

It is the tradition in many of our Vedanta centres in the West to have music before and after the Sunday lectures. Swami Prabhavananda, founder of the Vedanta Society of Southern California, said that the choir song before his Sunday lecture concentrated the minds of the congregation and created an atmosphere. A mood of serenity and devotion seems appropriate for most services, depending on the subject of the lecture.

Music can be a great help to us in our Godward path, but it should not take the place of other spiritual practices. Music is but one of the paths that can point us towards the Great Silence that is God.

15
Music for Personal Development

SWAMI VEETAMOHANANDA

Any art is a product of the collective consciousness of a society. It varies from one society to another and confers them distinctiveness. Each member of a society shares a common taste but not equally. Its intensification demands consciousness of it. The result of this intensification is greater mental refinement, enlarged vision, susceptibility and sensitiveness to the values which help us to ascend to a higher plane. The art-experience then deepens and broadens.

Every individual has two aspects: inward and outward. The former is related to aesthetics; the latter, to reasoning through the intellect. The balance between the two gives equilibrium and consistency to life. A good taste is an accomplishment of a rich inner life. It helps in a better orientation of the self to the external world. In other words, it promotes a simultaneous growth of both individual and society.

Music is an expressional mode of any culture. Let me speak about Indian music. It has four fundamental concepts: melody (rāga), rhythm (tāla), song, and the accompaniment or the instruments.

Whoever has heard Indian music in any form has heard about rāga or melody. How to explain or describe 'melody'? Take, for instance, a painting. A painting is, we may say, music for the eyes. A painting has in it figures or images, the different colours, etc., and all these put together make the painting attractive. In the same way, music also has its melody, rhythm, song, and the accompaniment.

Let me give another example: alphabets make a word, words make phrases, phrases put together give an idea of what we want to describe. In the same way, music has its notes. The notes are put together and are used according to the mood of the singer; that creates a melody. This melody is joined or put to express one's feelings through a song, and when the song is sung with melody and rhythm, it gives the needed feeling, it gives the needed 'picture' of one's idea.

What is meant by tāla or rhythm? Tāla is the unit of measuring a song, just as a metre is the measuring-unit of distance. The structure of each tāla is fixed and is different in different tālas. It repeats on and on like a spiral from the beginning to the end of a song. It determines both an individual event and corresponding events at any given moment. Here, by song is meant varied strips of compositions. They have different names such as ālāpa, dhrupada, ṭhumari, tarāna. In the southern school of music, they are called varṇa, kṛti, tillānā, etc.

The instruments are of different kinds like tānpurā, vīṇā, flute, mṛdaṅga, sitār, sāraṅgi, sarod, tablā, and so on. There are also modern instruments like violin, saxophone, clarinette, and mandolin.

Now to come to the components of musical experience. Indian music has generally two components: one is words, and the other is elements of melody. One who composes both is called vādyakara. The word-component contains both eternal values and emotion. It includes precepts of devotion, ethics, philosophy, social and cultural values, or the expression of sentiments like erotics, valour, pity, etc. In every pattern of music, the essence (*rasa*) is the autonomous aspect of music. It is absolute or pure in such creative elements as the development of a melody (rāga-ālāpanam), or an imaginary development of a melody (kalpanā-svara). It constitutes the actual meaning of music. Both words and essence mixed in a song in different proportions give a complex experience. While words dominate in some songs, the essence dominates in others. Both are important. The music which has words predominant has literary value. The essence-dominating music has musical value as well as literary value.

The musical experience occurs in us on four different planes. First is the physical response. When we hear good music, we start nodding our head, clapping our hands, or we beat time, sometimes we exclaim, or show our pleasure or express our emotion through tears.

The second experience is the mental response that affects us emotionally. It affects the 'inner environment,' producing sentiments of sorrow, pity, eroticism, etc. This can happen due to the words of the song as well.

The third experience is the intellectual or analytical response. It produces a conscious grasp of the aesthetic elements and the technique in both the essence and the words of the song or the music.

The fourth experience is the transcendental response in which the form of aesthetic beauty is realized. This is the highest plane of experience, the *pure* experience. This experience comes to us only when we dive deep into the very soul of music. We must be identified totally with the emotion (bhāva), melody (rāga), and rhythm (tāla).

Music can be made a channel for the expression of our emotions or sentiments. These are classically described as nine in number. One is *śṛṅgāra* or beauty; the second is *hāsya* or comedy, it makes you laugh; third, *karuṇā,* lamenting; fourth, raudra, attacking; vīra is valour; the next one is *bhayānaka,* fearful; then comes *bibhatsa,* ridiculous; and the last one is *adbhuta,* surprising.

To these sentiments, two more are sometimes added: *vātsalya,* tenderness, and *śānta,* calmness. From these nine sentiments, eight aesthetic moods *(bhāva)* originate. They also can be expressed through music. One is affection; second is laughter; third is grief; fourth, anger; fifth is ridicule; sixth, fear; seventh, hatred; and the last one is surprise. This is what makes music so important for the development of our personality. We can easily transform our emotions through it. Music helps us to be creative.

Every aspect of life demands certain methods and disciplines. Music also has its method of learning. Only when we express music systematically does it give us the joy of creativity. The joy of *listening* to music can be had only when we tune our mind to the musician's level of consciousness. When we listen to a singer, the direct vibration of the singer touches us and gives us joy. Listening to tapes or records we don't get this kind of direct vibration; we get only the joy emanating from the essence of the music.

Music is a system of education in itself. It imparts knowledge and experience. It animates and elevates our levels of consciousness. It makes our whole life sweet, both outside and inside. Music has the capacity to go deep and transform the life of a spiritual seeker. It can stimulate the seeker's quest to solve the mystery of life. Music broadens our mind and intellect. It enlightens our soul and prepares it to realize the true import of life and art. We should not remain contented with the practice of hearing melodies formed out of a combination and permutation of tunes. We should dive deep into the very core of the melody.

Music is a gift or a boon to us all because it comforts our mind and helps it to concentrate and meditate upon a universal idea or ideal. It frees us from false knowledge and ignorance, and gives us peace and happiness even in our everyday life.

16
Musicians and Their Music

RAJKUMAR BHARATHI

Human life looks mundane outwardly, but inwardly it is rich. We know of the lives of great men and women who led exemplary lives. It is they who have handed down noble values to posterity. These values give a person his or her personality. Values cannot be explained. They have to be experienced.

What I have said above is just to 'tune' myself as well you, readers, to the values of music. The capacity of the mind to tune itself to various moods and messages and persons is acquired by listening to good music.

Music is my very breath. It has influenced in a big way the pattern of my life. I feel blessed that God has made me a musician. How much peace and harmony music has brought to the world! Music is, no doubt, a pleasing experience for the ear. The ear *hears* music, but the soul *enjoys* it. Whether music can provide a temporary 'kick' lasting for a short period of time provoking the nervous system to execute violent body-movements or whether music can create a sense of utmost peace and bliss depends on the quality of music and its value.

To understand the value of anything, we need a Master, or guru. In music the guru-sishya (teacher-disciple) relation is a divine one. In one of his compositions, saint-composer Muthuswamy Dikshitar hails Goddess Parvati as *Guru-śiṣya rūpa-dhāriṇī,* 'One who has taken the form of both teacher and disciple.'

The guru first disciplines the student outwardly. The guru's competence has an impact on the student's mind. Initially the music lessons become a routine exercise. We can call this the conditioning process. Apart from the guru, the support of parents and the nature of the surroundings are also very important for the student. The student gets convinced that he or she is learning something valuable and soon gets attached to music. The guru continues to guide the student. The student's unflinching faith in the guru starts yielding results. The student learns many musical compositions. He or she soon gets to know of the history of music, its uniqueness, its value in society, its tempering effect on the human mind, etc. This is a fairly long process running into many years. This is the period when the guru-sishya bond gets strengthened.

I have had the blessed good fortune of learning music from several renowned teachers, beginning with my own mother. They all taught me the intricate nuances of music.

They taught me to *enjoy* music. How can I explain this enjoyment! It is impossible to put it into words. To *feel* God in the divine vibrations of music is the urge that my gurus have kindled in me.

Music is a divine gift. Its value has to be clearly understood by professional musicians. Oftentimes, professionalism is marred by the ego element and commercial exploitation. Nevertheless, a musician cannot afford to neglect the values of music. A true professional always has a great love for his art. So a true musician would never do anything that tends to cheapen the taste and lower the quality of music.

Professional musicians earn their livelihood through music, but they also render different types of services. There are occasions when money is not the criterion but only service. For example, the famous Tyagaraja Aradhana festival at Thiruvaiyaru near Tanjore in Tamil Nadu. It is a holy occasion when musicians come together and offer their homage to the great saint-composer Tyagaraja. Music-lovers gather in huge numbers and the entire region is filled with pure vibrations.

The great saint-composers of our country—like Purandara Dasa, Kanaka Dasa, Tyagaraja, Dikshitar, Shyama Sastry, Annamacharya, Tulsi Das, Kabir Das, Jayadeva—had no mercenary motive. They sang out of devotion to God. Music flowed in them due to God's grace and they were fully aware of this. That is why they could create immortal compositions which are vibrant even today and would be so for ever. We musicians make our living singing the compositions of these saints.

Some musicians render another service: teaching. Teaching is one of the noblest professions. Teaching music is one way of expressing gratitude to the art. This helps in the propagation of the knowledge of music and leads to survival of the art through ages. There has to be real transmission of knowledge. This become possible only when the musician-teacher realizes that he or she is a mere tool in the hands of the Creator.

Total surrender to God helps the musician to communicate well with his or her listeners. To deal with the masses one has to be like a seasoned teacher handling young children in the class. Some children may be obedient, intelligent, and cooperative; some others may be naughty, dull, and unwilling to obey. A good teacher handles all these children skilfully and turns out wonderful students. Same is the case in music. The audience may be of many types—elite, commonplace, mediocre. How should a musician handle them? First of all, the musician himself has to enjoy his music. This definitely has a great influence on the audience. The musician who enjoys singing takes the audience along with him. Some people think that Carnatic music is not for the masses. This is true to some extent, but that does not mean we should discard classical music and pander to popular tastes. Let me narrate an incident from my own career.

Some years ago I went to Tiruppur in Tamil Nadu to give a Carnatic music concert in a temple. In Tiruppur, at that time, Carnatic music had little recognition. I started the concert and, when I was singing the first piece, someone passed a slip of paper to my mridanga-player, even as he was playing it. I finished the first item and then looked at that slip. It said, 'Please stop singing Carnatic music. Sing light music.' I called the person who gave it and asked him who had sent the slip and why. He replied that the secretary of the organization (who had invited me) had written the note because there were many school children among the audience who knew nothing about Carnatic music and that they would go away. I can't explain how I felt at that time, but one thing I did: I totally surrendered myself to God. I calmly told the person to have a little patience. I then sang without elaborating technically some compositions in Tamil including many songs of my illustrious great-grandfather Subramanya Bharathi. That clicked! The audience began to appreciate the songs. I then gradually elaborated two or three items and the audience sat spellbound. When the programme concluded, the organizers were greatly apologetic about the slip of paper and insisted that the audience should attend only such types of concerts in future. God protected me. Music saved me. And music won for itself.

Some people like fun, and some forms of music provide that too. I am not critical of these forms of music. But fun is just a passing feature. The mind does not get elevated by that kind of music, accompanying which there may be vigorous dancing and clapping. But how does it all end? In exhaustion. The body gets totally tired and the mind gets confused. On the other hand, the effect of good, devotional, elevating music is so different! It produces peace, joy and harmony in both body and mind. How transcendent that feeling is! That is why we must recognize the distinction between good taste and bad taste. The musician's duty to the masses lies in generating a good taste in them.

Music radiates serenity and joy. When a musician enjoys sedately while performing, then the masses respond accordingly. If we musicians sing and dance violently, the masses respond to that too. So we cannot blame the masses; they are only following the current. It is the musician's duty and responsibility to lead others in the proper direction; they must simultaneously entertain, educate, and elevate the masses. Such efforts will lead to unity and harmony in society.

Sometimes we hear people in India lamenting that our music is 'gone and lost.' Well, our music has a divine source, so we need not worry. Our music will take care of its own survival. At times, out of love for music, we musicians tend to think that we are responsible for its survival. That is a totally wrong and egoistic feeling. On the contrary, it is music which is responsible for *our* survival. Let us understand this well and our music will always keep us happy and fulfilled.

17

The Values of an Actor

ALAN ARKIN

Some years ago I was starring in a film that spoke eloquently of the plight of Puerto Ricans in the United States. The basic theme was man's inhumanity to man, and I was deeply proud to be connected with the project. It was exactly the kind of film I'd always dreamed of making. In the script there was a scene which involved the decapitation of a pigeon. It was an important scene, and its violence had meaning in the context of the film.

Minutes before the scene was to be shot I discovered that a real pigeon was going to be used and that its head would actually be cut off. I was shocked and enraged, and in this state I confronted the producers. I threatened them, I screamed obscenities at them, and ultimately bullied them into finding another method for depicting the scene, which they did grudgingly, unhappy about slowing down the schedule, but more afraid of my rage.

After I cooled down and had a chance to think about what had taken place, I was struck by the several levels of irony in the event. Here was a scene devoted to pointing a finger at man's barbarity, and in depicting it we were using the same cruel methods we were decrying in the script! To add to the knot of ironies, to stop the producers' mindlessness and cruelty I flew into a violent rage, adding my own brand of cruelty to the stew we were concocting. Layer upon layer of confusion. The moment resounded in me for a long time.

It was a period in my life when I was beginning the long look inward, and as a result of this episode and other similar situations, I came to see that the great truths I hoped to bring to my audiences were not alive in me. Ethical questions began to arise, and still do. I know there is no place in my life for violence. But is there a place for violence in films? Can I be associated with such films? The answer comes from the same place that all true answers come from. What is the spirit of the piece? Does the violence serve the integrity of the work? Does the work somehow serve us? Are the writers and director infatuated with violence or do they weep at the thought of hurting someone? Shakespeare's works are filled with violence, but we always sense his vantage point, the necessity and the context. We never feel him using violence to vent his own rage.

Values in the arts seem to be more ephemeral than in other areas of our life. For example, if I make chairs, then at least on the surface my ethical task seems simple. There are tangible results that even the most modest chair-builder must adhere to. The chair must support weight. It should last. The chair should be free from splinters. All pretty obvious and hard to argue with. On the surface it seems easy to evaluate this type of work. But in order for the carpenter to consider these issues fully, he must have a sense of love for the wood, the screws, the glue, and the saw. Otherwise making the chair will be a task to finish as quickly as possible and the shoddiness of the work will show sooner or later. Mistakes will be made and the chair will not have the desired integrity.

In the theatre and in film it's more difficult to define the task. Not to bore the audience seems to be a good goal, but who is the audience? And at what lengths do we go not to bore him? What bores one person will delight someone else. And what are the materials we work with? We can do without a stage, sometimes without lights, sometimes even without a script. In movies, with the exception of a camera and a roll of film the same is true. The basic elements that are necessary are some kind of story, a few people to tell it, and an attempt to communicate something. But the substance of what we are communicating is the basis of an argument that can go on forever.

What I have come to believe is that the underlying event of every theatrical enterprize—more important than the varieties of equipment, the quality of the material, and varieties of talents involved—must always be the relationships with the people we are working with. Too often we have the tendency to sacrifice the life in front of us for the imaginary life of the script. But our feeling for people can't be imaginary or theoretical. It has to be in evidence to the living people immediately in front of us. We must care for them more than the characters in our scripts. We must love them, respond to them, give them our attention and enjoy them, and this will spill over into our work on the scripts. It will illuminate the text, give it spontaneity and depth, and bring joy to the work-process, and the audiences will sense it and they will remember with an aching joy. I can't tell you the number of times strangers come up to me and ask, 'In such and such a film, were you having as wonderful a time as it looked?' Invariably my answer is yes. The audiences seem to have an unfailing instinct for sensing the projects that worked—the projects that were fulfilling for those who made it, the projects that had a sense of community and joy.

When I was a young student of acting, I often became lost in the complexities of how to create a character. Through the help of my wonderful teacher I slowly developed a series of techniques that gave me the feeling of being centred while on stage. When I applied these techniques well, they gave me a sense of freedom within the character and took away my self-consciousness about being in front of an audience. These techniques stood me in good stead for many decades, and they worked so well that after a while they stopped being techniques and turned into rules.

These rules held fast till I was well into my forties, when I suddenly realized that these laws I'd invented had to some extent blinded me to human feeling. This came as a great shock because I grew up with a belief that theatre and film were wonderful arenas for teaching. For showing people the depth and breadth of the human condition, the possibilities for change; for growth; for joy; for examining other cultures and learning from their differences and similarities. Most of us like to have slogans to live by. Rules and regulations for each occasion that, if not handed down to us, we make up for ourselves. It keeps the world from seeming random and chaotic. With these rules, we gain a semblance of control. They can be gentle rules or harsh rules, or anything in the spectrum, but what I have learned—if I have learned anything—is that the rules break down. No matter how beautiful or perfect the axiom, there are times in our lives when we are not served by them.

The universe demands that we be made flexible. That we examine our lives from the context of the moment. From the experience right before our eyes, and not from our successes or failures of yesterday, or the truths of last year. As an actor and director I am constantly faced with this juggling act. The choices I made in my work a few years ago no longer feel alive. The rules I made for honest work yesterday are lies today. Through time I have learned to be grateful for this and not be frightened, because the result I see is this: the extent that I can make this idea live and breathe in me, is the exact extent that I am a dynamic force as an actor. I have to be a changing, growing organism, rather than a rigid system of old decisions made to keep myself in check. Rule-making is nothing but a chain around the neck to give oneself the illusion of order. But this order is not the order of nature in which change is the one constant we have to trust.

I was once offered a project that I felt ambivalent towards and, as I did when faced with most confusions, I brought it to my Guru. I told him about the script and he immediately asked, 'What is the piece serving?' I had to answer that I didn't know. I thought I could bring some life to the part, but that the script was poorly written and thin. 'If you can bring life to the part you will be serving the piece,' my Guru answered, 'and you will be feeding your family.' That ended the conversation.

As an actor I am at the mercy of the scripts I am offered. Sometimes it's a feast and sometimes it's pretty thin stuff. When the offering is not to my liking I have the choice to dismiss it, sulk in a corner or even make chairs, but I prefer to work at what I know; grateful when I am offered something grand and willing to struggle for coherence with something pedestrian. In each case I make the attempt to make an offering to someone. To another actor on the set, to someone on the crew, to the script, to the character—at the very least, to put food on the table for my family.

18
Values in Journalism

GUY E. OLSON

A gruesome story that first surfaced in 1987 has been repeated by news media throughout Latin America and in Europe, East Asia, and South Asia, including India. It concerns the kidnapping or adoption of infants and children in poor countries and the butchering of them so that their body organs can be used to save the lives of patients in America and other wealthy countries.

There is a major problem with this continuing story. It has yet to be proven to be true. For some eight years now, much of the world press, along with the public that it serves, has been duped by a rumour that just won't go away. The U.S. Information Agency made an exhaustive inquiry and submitted a report to the United Nations that said: 'No government, international body, non-governmental organization, or investigative journalist has ever produced any credible evidence to substantiate this story...' *Newsweek* magazine recently reported on its own investigation into the story, concluding: 'All it lacks is a single cold cadaver.'

The perpetuation of this unfounded rumour points up the failure of many press organs around the world to adhere to two of the most cherished values of professional journalism: truth and accuracy.

Carelessness is the root cause of most false or inaccurate news stories, but many other factors can contribute to the problem. Pressures applied by advertisers, government, political organizations, business, and other powerful institutions—including the press itself—are examples. The role that sensationalism plays in selling a news product, be it a newspaper or a television broadcast, is certainly another factor, and one that no doubt can be linked to the body-parts story.

Purposeful Values

TRUTH AND ACCURACY are the foundation pillars of good journalism and essential to the journalist's mission to serve the public's need to know and understand the issues of the day that affect people's lives and welfare. But there are several other values as well that I would briefly like to discuss. Though my observations are largely informed by the conditions of journalism as practised in the United States, I would contend that—with the possible exception of a few lingering proponents of the discredited idea of a 'new world information order'—they are values shared by professional journalists around the world.

One is RESPONSIBILITY. This value works on several levels. To serve the public's need to know, the journalist must take responsibility for scrutinizing the forces of power in society—government and business among them—whose actions and decisions can materially affect our lives. On another level, the journalist must take responsibility for the facts that he/she reports and the conclusions he/she reaches.

The exercise of GOOD JUDGMENT is part and parcel of this responsibility. What is and is not news is something always open to debate. A century ago the city editor of the *New York Sun* gave a definition that has since entered the annals of aphorisms: 'When a dog bites a man, that's not news. When a man bites a dog, *that's* news.'

That doesn't quite help us deal with what has become a growing preoccupation of the press—prying into the private affairs of public persons. In recent years a debate has been going on within the journalism community over the relevance that such things as physical condition and personal morality have for an individual's capacity to serve in a public position. The role of the press in this regard is something that may never be defined to the satisfaction of all concerned.

INDEPENDENCE is essential if the journalist is to be trusted as a purveyor of truth and accuracy. This means avoiding impropriety as well as the appearance of impropriety. Many news organizations go to great lengths to ensure the independence of their personnel. Reporters for the *Wall*

Street Journal, for instance, are strictly forbidden from accepting gifts of any kind from the businesses they cover, regardless of value.

Major newspapers such as the *New York Times* and the *Washington Post* forbid their theatre critics from accepting free tickets to performances or their travel writers from taking trips paid for by the tourist industry. Less financially endowed news organizations, however, find it difficult, if not impossible, to abide by these standards. Consequently, compromises are made. Nevertheless, reporters covering affairs of government and business should scrupulously avoid any taint of partiality.

FAIR PLAY is closely related to impartiality. Journalists need to respect the rights of those whom they write about, abide by standards of common decency, and identify their sources. Promising confidentiality to a news source is sometimes necessary—and in the public's interest—in order to get a story. When given, confidentiality should be honoured. But it should be given sparingly and only when absolutely necessary. Frequent and gratuitous use of confidential sources only erodes the credibility of the reporter and of journalism in general. Someone who doesn't want to be identified as a news source may have ulterior motives that are less than honourable.

The journalist should keep a large dollop of SCEPTICISM in his or her bag of values. Question everything, but in doing so, avoid cynicism, a self-defeating quality that sticks to some reporters like chewing gum to the sole of a shoe. Cynicism is insidious because it leads to anomie and alienation and, consequently, the loss of values.

The Impossible Value?

The penultimate value or standard that I want to mention is often the one mentioned first, OBJECTIVITY. It's also the one subject to the most debate. Objectivity means the absence of emotion or personal prejudice, and these are qualities that are often difficult or impossible for a journalist in the line of duty to maintain.

How can one expect a reporter exposed to the bloodshed of war or the devastation that attends a natural calamity such as an earthquake to remain emotionally detached? Eliminating prejudice is a praiseworthy goal. In fact, to me personally, as a member of the Baha'i Faith, it is of critical importance to the growth of mankind. I see it as the core cause of the national, religious, and ethnic conflicts that have broken out all over the world in recent years. Until we human beings eliminate our prejudices, we will not have peace and unity in this world.

Now, in telling you this, I have revealed a personal value of my own that I try, with only partial success, to abide by. We all have personal values, journalists included. Therefore, pure objectivity is quite impossible—and in the final analysis, undesirable—to have. In his book, *Deciding What's News,* Herbert Gans writes:

'Journalists try hard to be objective, but neither they nor anyone else can in the end proceed without values. Furthermore, reality judgments are never altogether divorced from values... If a news story deals with activities which are generally considered undesirable and whose descriptions contain negative connotations, then the story implicitly expresses a value about what is desirable... When a story reports that a politician has been charged with corruption, it suggests, *sotto voce,* that corruption is bad and that politicians should be honest.'

This, then, explains why most of the news we read is bad. Either people have done something that violates one or more of the values that society cherishes, or there has been a tragedy of some kind. The French writer Paul Valery once said: 'If some great catastrophe is not announced every morning, we feel a certain void. "Nothing in the paper today," we sigh.'

One of the catastrophes that greeted newspaper readers and television viewers several months ago was the terrorist bombing of a federal government building in Oklahoma City, Oklahoma. One of the rescue workers who put their lives on the line in the search for survivors was Rebecca Anderson, a nurse and a mother of four children. She was hit by a piece of concrete in the effort and later died. Her well-documented story offers a counterpoint to the undocumented anecdote with which I began this article:

Anderson had signed a pledge card stating that upon death, any of her organs could be transplanted to the body of anyone else. Immediately after she died, doctors took her heart to save the life of a man in Oklahoma and one of her kidneys to save the life of a woman in New Mexico.

And so out of a story of abject cruelty and tragedy came a very different story of goodness and generosity, of ultimate sacrifice. Which leads me to conclude with a call for a final value: That the journalist—amidst the crimes, scandals, political machinations, economic developments, business reports, and other items that dominate his or her attention—search for those stories that inspire us, that confirm for us, as in the story of Rebecca Anderson, the inherent goodness of our fellow human beings. For lack of a better word I will call this value UPLIFTMENT.

In 1897, a young girl wrote a letter to the editor of the *New York Sun* saying that some of her playmates had told her there was no Santa Claus. She asked the *Sun* to tell her the truth. The editor took advantage of the letter to inspire readers with what probably is the most widely quoted newspaper editorial ever written:

'Virginia, your little friends are wrong. They have been affected by the scepticism of a sceptical age. They do not believe except what they see... Yes, Virginia, there is a Santa Claus. He exists as certainly as love and generosity and devotion exist, and you know that they abound and give to. your life its highest beauty and joy... The most real things in the world are those that neither children nor men can see.'

Love, generosity, devotion, beauty, joy—they are all there for us to see, and journalists are eminently suited to show them to us, if only they will look for them.

19

Newspeople and News-consumers

JEAN-MARC OHLMANN

Novelty is what attracts many a journalist in his or her career. Is novelty a value? At first sight, it seems to be just the opposite of a never-changing, eternal, deep-rooted value. We shall try to answer this question after having observed the daily work of a journalist within his or her field of interest.

A journalist is hunting for novelty everywhere or, at least, trying to find a new angle of view at old things in order to attract his reader or listener or spectator. We find a lot of differences among the different media, but we can overlook them here. We shall also reduce the scope of this essay to general information and leave aside specialized information, where values have little specific impact. We shall study the different values in journalism one by one, by examining thoroughly the way of working in this profession, then its historical evolution, and the general trends which can forecast the future.

Every day the common journalist is overwhelmed by masses of information from varied sources, much more than he needs. His first task is to select them according to the general policy laid down by his employer and also depending on their novelty or interest. Beyond the demands of the medium, this never innocent selection is deeply connected with the general values of the society the journalist is living in, so it has very little to do with personal values. Let's remember that the journalist, or his employer, does a kind of classification which is called the hierarchy of information. From different categories he selects only the 'top events.' He then considers the suitableness of the form and the length of the material and checks that the message answers to the fundamental rules known as the 5-W's: What? Who? When? Why? Where? completed by the background of the event and, if possible, by attractive anecdotes. Up to that point the journalist is a specialized worker in information-business, where information is a product like any other and does not need any peculiar values other than common professional skill, even his own tastes or concerns play little role. The work of a great majority of journalists does not go beyond that point.

Most of the time the 'product', merely a support for advertisement, has been prepared by a news agency or a communication office—private or public—and can be used after minor editing. With the use of modern technologies, processors and interconnected networks especially, journalists have increasingly become links in a chain which is also shaped by its smaller elements: desk journalism and institutional journalism.

This chain is supplied, for a major part, by the news agencies' reporters whose role is also technical. They collect the information from direct sources and are supposed to check it. We can find here a first kind of value, even if the truth they are looking for cannot be called a philosophical or religious truth. It is only a causal, rational truth, or at least a probable truth, based on the likelihood of an event and the credibility of the sources. Anyway, the news agency reporter is supposed to deliver a strong product to all media around the world. All he can do is give different versions of an event. He can hardly express his doubts if he has any or say 'I don't know' when he doesn't.

For a happy few among the journalists, the work is sometimes different and requires further skills. These are usually the well-known, well-established reporters who contribute for the major part of most media image. The work of such a journalist is closer to the mythological and glamorous image. He has a strong position and can legitimately claim more liberty within the several limits determined by the environment, the employer, the consumers, and the announcers of his medium. His work consists mainly in transforming or commenting on the news agencies' material. He can correct the errors or improve the presentation through his experience and intuition, or he may even distort the material through his personal prejudices, political opinions and, last but not least, his own auto-censorship. He may work abroad on direct sources, as a high profile reporter, or more commonly, in his own area, collecting information, investigating—this is very rare in Europe—or interviewing varied personalities. For all these activities, integrity, independence, ever-fresh curiosity, strength of character, firmness, courage and such other qualities are required. To find all these in any one person is difficult. There is, moreover, an unavoidable tension when these qualities are made to coexist along with departmental politicking necessary to keep on top of what has more and more the characteristics of a star-system. These journalists belong to an inner circle of other stars in political, financial, economic, cultural fields with whom they talk sometimes more often 'off the record' than 'on the record.' This is the reason why cant language prevails instead of no-holds-barred interviews.

We find, of course, some exceptions in this oversimplified outline. A few journalists do a really good job for a time, but they usually have little impact on the general trend. And, in the long run, even with the best motivation, it is impossible for them to avoid dancing along a very blurred ethical borderline. There are also what is called 'scandals' revealed by the press, but most of the time journalists are manipulated in some way or other by the very people who supply the information. A scandal usually comes before the public eye only when it is beneficial to someone. That is the way through which sometimes misdeeds get the exciting status of 'novelty.'

This is not a terribly inspiring state of affairs, but as the press is a faithful mirror of society, we find in journalism the values that contemporary society cherishes. We must remember that reporters are not the seekers of the unfound new values, or the knights of the modern Grail quest. The mythical image of the reporter is still woven by those illusions. A young journalist's eyes are opened not long after beginning the career when he or she learns the 'number of deads/km' law. This law states that the importance of an event is directly proportional to the number of people killed and the relative proximity of its occurrence. This unwritten law of sensationalism is so openly cynical that it is the most innocuous among all the rules presiding over the hierarchy of information.

Besides proximity of the event, if the news item has elements of bloodshed, hatred, hard competition, and sex, it makes headlines. The emphasis on sensationalism is the result of the craze for novelty. This is only a sophisticated quest for sensuality and is thus definitely out of the field of values. Worse, this quest for novelty prevents the journalists from seeing the basic background and forces them away to suggest new solutions without being able to understand a problem or an event. This is why the more people are informed, the less they understand anything, either about the external world or about themselves.

The quest for novelty, this curiosity, is an inheritance from the old Greeks and their eagerness to change the world. It is a mark of our civilization of progress. 'What's new?' means 'What's better?' or 'What has been improved today?' The answer is always about the worsened, the wrong, in a world where new problems arise before the current ones are solved. Born in a world of violence, of strong opposition to everything ancient, modern journalism focuses itself on what is wrong in this world, on the conflicts, on the many defects, because of their sensationalism and the natural propensity of human nature for gossip and seeing other people's defects. Through this deforming mirror effect, journalism appears to increase the decay in society and to support wrong values, among which perversion of taste is high up on the list.

Journalism has pushed humanity in a kind of everlasting drama which has none of the appeasing effects of the 'artistic drama' as defined by Aristotle under the term 'catharsis'. A few attempts have been made to reverse the trend, but it is impossible for journalism to deal with such subjects as trains arriving on time or the blooming of flowers. It would need other skills and minds far away from the journalistic universe of rationalism: the poetic intellect which disappeared under the scorn of the utilitarians.

The development of journalism is closely linked with the emergence of public opinion as a ruling power, when the old traditional values began to be neglected and then given up. Journalism has become an important institution of democracy through transparency and freedom of information. It has become what is known as the Fourth Estate. Naturally, it is not free from common institutional evils such as unbridled ambitions, petty politicking, and corruption. Like any other business, its primary aim is money-making. This development has affected the flowering of true democracy and justice. For example, political leaders generally take up only such issues and problems as are brought to light by the strong urging of the media.

Journalism is still very young and, unless there is a cultural revolution amongst its consumers, it will not mature in spite of—or because of—the worldwide interconnected network, the growing numbers of media, and the technological progress. Perhaps a revolution will come nevertheless out of some unexpected but predictable use of technology—I mean, out of what is called the multimedia-processing, just arriving on the scene. With it every consumer will be able to have access to any information or image-bank or network, make his own home-news, and broadcast them. This might announce the end of journalism as a 'caste' of specialized worker and the beginning of a maturation of news-consumers.

Meanwhile, what can a Vedanta student or someone with a religious attitude do in such a profession? Those connected with a church or sect can work in the media linked with their church or sect. Religious publications are much fewer in Europe than in India. Vedanta students can manage to find a sort of niche somewhere and to do their work as honestly as possible, remembering always that nothing is perfect in God's līlā. They can also look upon information as the ever-changing deceitful mask of māyā—or the play of the Divine Mother, who is the Weaver-of-the-news, and pay a tribute to Her.

20
Journalism and Power

ANN LOUISE BARDACH

I can make no claims for motives of altruism in my work: only curiosity. And if there has been any cohesive theme to my work it has been around power and powerlessness. I have always been fascinated by the uses and misuses of power—who has it, who doesn't, what people will do to get it, and what they do with it once they have it. No doubt, it was my own sense of powerlessness in a world of impossible randomness that propelled me towards journalism. If I could have no control over my family, my community, my country, or my planet, then at least I could gleam the secrets directly from those that did and did not. Of course, journalism with its access to the powerful is a form of power in itself and I cannot deny the adrenalized headiness that comes with the job.

Reporting is my antidote for my feelings of helplessness, my lack of power. It is the way I contribute to a seemingly indifferent universe. Journalism has the power of throwing a magical spotlight on its subjects—making the unseen, seen, the unheard, heard, the ignored, noted. It can be an enormously potent force, a power that must be used with judicious care. Indeed, it is a sacred trust. Although I appreciate and admire reporters who day in and day out neutrally record the day's events, it is not what I do. I write only about people, events, stories that I care deeply about. If nothing else, I know I will need to summon enough passion to see me through the process: the legwork, the research, the often humiliating hustle of nailing down interviews—before one gets to do a lick of writing. Generally speaking, I write about somebody or something when I can no longer contain my own curiosity or outrage.

While I have my share of misgivings about what's currently being called advocacy journalism, neither do I come to a story as a *tabula rasa.* What the French call *engage*—a commitment to certain social and ethical values—is a fair description of how and what I do. However, whatever prior opinions I may hold are invariably shattered. Stories, like people, are always complex matters. Rarely is a villain only a villain, a murderer only a murderer, a revolutionary only a revolutionary. As the cliché goes, 'every killer is some mother's son.' Fidel Castro is and has been at various times a revolutionary, coward, tyrant, visionary, a monster, and so on.

Always I am surprised and disappointed in unforseen ways. The Chiapan peasant leader Subcomandante Marcos, who comes as close to a hero as I expect to meet in my life, floored me with his schoolboy humour. When asked by a human rights activist who accompanied me, what provisions he most needed in his jungle hideout, he responded, 'an inflatable sex doll.' Nor will I ever forget Benazir Bhutto strutting into her sister's Knightsbridge flat decked out in a full length sable to discuss women's rights with me or the single-minded ruthlessness of Turkey's Tansu Ciller so chillingly at odds with her blonde Gidget-friendly looks. I was stunned to learn that the sheriff who 'escorted' me out of the town of Lynch, Virginia in 1978 was a Klansman. Nor was I quite prepared to discover the supremacy of fashion—even in the rain forest of Chiapas where two scrawny Zapatista soldiers demanded my $280 designer combat boots. When I suggested that they take something else—namely, some more food—they smiled and raised their rifles, reminding me who was in charge. Then there was the dour Saudi scholar Mai Yamani who touched my arm at the conclusion of our interview and asked, 'Do you like flamenco dancing? It's my passion. I dance five nights a week.' And she began to dance.

Even the most chillingly bleak stories have stunned me with curious paradoxes and surprises. How does one explain, for example, how a region such as the Middle East, notorious for its repression of women, has produced three women presidents/prime ministers while the United States has yet to elect one. Could it be that the most astute students of power are its victims as Yeats mused about Zeus' rape of Leda, 'Did she put on his power before the indifferent beak let her drop.'

As for method, I find that the more empathetic I am with my subject, no matter what deeds or crimes he or she may have committed, the more successful I am. When I am interviewing the powerful, the rich or the very famous, sometimes the only way I can calm my nerves and ego is to repeat to myself mantra-like, 'I'm here to be of love and service.' Amazingly, it relieves me of my distracting self-obsessiveness and puts the focus directly on the subject, where it should be. When I am covering disasters, accidents, murders and general wretched of the earth, I am almost always reminded that 'there but for the grace of God go I.' Always, the challenge is not to judge, but to observe with compassion and carry the story back to you.

21

Values in Writing for Children

BARBARA DANA

One of the first things that attracted me to writing for children was that I could write about things I wanted to write about. Another thing was that I wouldn't have to write about things I didn't want to write about. The things I wanted to write about included: hope; charity; listening to one's inner voice; the lives of animals; the importance of small things; reaping what you sow; not running with the pack; seeing humour in the way things are usually done; heroism; daring; responsibility; and a connection between all forms of life. The things I didn't want to write about included: sex; violence; drugs; and politics. So writing for children seemed a perfect work for me.

There were other reasons I began to write for children. I remember my childhood vividly. I find it a truly interesting time. Also, when I began writing for children I felt more like a child than a grown-up. At fifty-four I still feel that way, which either means that I'm stunted in my growth, or that the way I feel now is the way people feel when they're supposedly grown-up. Or maybe both. Perhaps, my conception of what it feels like to be a grown-up is incorrect, or maybe the way it feels to be a grown-up is relative.

In looking at my reasons for wanting to write for children I think the main reason is that I can express life's values, as I feel them in my work. I can spend precious time each day expressing what I feel is important. This is a great blessing.

When you write for children it's considered a good thing to be hopeful. It's all right to suggest that there's a way out, that hard work pays off, that small things matter, that sacrifice can lead to joy. In writing for adults these things are not so highly thought of. They're often considered unrealistic, or boring, or naïve, or worse yet, not commercial enough to make any money. Sadly, this last point is often true.

I'm not sure why there appears to be this double standard. A lot of times I hear adults say they long to read books and see films containing positive and hopeful values. They say they're tired of all the sex and violence and meaningless car chases. They don't want to read about more buildings being blown up, about more people being murdered, or dying from taking too many drugs. They long for stories about people being good to each other, about individuals overcoming struggles, loving each other, growing, learning to laugh, and experiencing joy. Still, modern novels and films like this for adults are few and far between. I know they exist, but they do seem to be in the minority.

It's as if the message is: Children should hear nice things. They're not ready yet to face reality, to concentrate on things as they really are, which is tough and brutal.

I can think of two comments to make about this. First of all, children face hard things all the time. Responsibility is tough. Sharing is tough. Death is tough. So is loss and change. Sometimes I think that themes like responsibility and sacrifice are harder for adults to take than themes like, say, 'Bad people you don't care about sometimes blow up a lot of trains filled with many kinds of people you don't care about.' May be all the violence and lack of real feeling in so many modern books and films is a kind of escape from some of the harsher realities like vulnerability, one's own death, or the weight of being dependable. I'm not sure.

Maybe the message is that children should hear nice things and adults shouldn't, or don't need to. Or maybe there is no message. Maybe it's just that books and films without a strong sense of values make more money, because for some reason, we need to experience a lot of random chaos. Maybe nobody believes that violence and indifference are particularly nourishing for anybody, but that where children are concerned we'd better give them what they should have and where adults are concerned 'money talks.'

I'm speaking in generalities. There are beautiful books written for people of all ages. And appreciated by them too. It just seems that in writing for children the acceptance of stories that speak of hope and kindness and positive outcomes is greater.

Charlotte Zolotow, my brilliant editor at Harper-Collins, also writes for children. Years ago she spoke to me about our work and what she treasures most about it. She said, 'Children are so open. They haven't decided what they feel about things yet. There's still a chance of reaching them.'

I knew what she meant. I seems to me that children have fewer prejudices than older people have. You can reach children with a thought, or an experience that may affect the way they feel about a thing for the rest of their lives. This makes the responsibility of writing for them overwhelming sometimes, but also deeply rewarding. The long hours I spend alone, writing, make sense to me. In addition to enjoying my work, I feel that the words set down can perhaps impact another person's life. This is a nourishing feeling.

My books, so far, seem to have a running theme. I didn't plan it this way, but in looking at my work I've noticed that each story seems to say the same thing: Listen to your inner voice; stick to your convictions even when everyone around you is telling you you're crazy; follow the dictates of your heart no matter how inconvenient. To me, the epitome of this point of view is dealt with in my book on Joan of Arc. Joan has always been my benchmark of courage and honesty and being true to one's self. In telling her story I got the chance to explore these qualities to their deepest roots.

The book I'm working on now has a different theme. It's about a young girl who was in an automobile accident as a small child and has to be in a wheelchair. She feels isolated from life, from other people, estranged even from herself. She is given a special dog who has been trained to help her get around, perform certain tasks and keep her company. Through her love for this dog and her devotion to his needs she grows happy and strong. The story deals with the power of love and devotion and how in surrendering to another's love for you, and in losing yourself in the service of another, you can grow and experience joy.

I feel grateful to be able to deal with these kinds of themes and to have my books published, but it's getting harder. When I started writing for children Charlotte would say things like, 'I don't know how well this book will sell, but it's about something important and it should be read.' You don't hear that now. You hear about marketing and sales and how well a book will translate to multimedia, but you don't hear much about content. This worries me. But hopefully, there's still time. Hopefully, people, including book publishers, still feel that children are the future of the world. That by exposing them to light-filled values one can positively affect the quality of future.

22
Values in the Medical Field

Dr. B. Ramamurthi

Thousands of years ago, when human civilization was in its infancy, people attempted to help a fellow being who was ill or injured and thus the practice of medicine was born. With experience accrued over generations, the art and science of medicine began to develop. In early history, doctoring the sick was a part-time occupation with few monetary benefits, except for gratitude sometimes expressed in terms of goods or money. Later, as the science grew, it became a full-time occupation and doctors had to be specially trained in the art and science of medicine. Medicine became a 'profession'. In ancient India the qualifications of a medical student and the medical teachers, as also their duties towards each other and to the public, were well-defined.

On graduation, the doctor took the oath of honesty, purity, etc., which stressed all the ethical values. Later, with Western medicine becoming popular in the country, the medical students were asked to take the Hippocratic Oath, which originated in Greece. The Hindu version of such an oath has been in existence long before the Hippocratic Oath. But most Indians have not heard about it or have forgotten it. Since Independence, this practice of Oath-taking has been given up in most places.

The training of the medical students and the oath that they took on graduation fully reflected the great ethical values that were instilled into all medical students and doctors. Thus medical ethics became the bedrock of medical practice and dharmic ideals prevailed. As regards remuneration for services rendered, this always took a secondary place. The medical students and the medical profession were indoctrinated with the principle that medical treatment is based on compassion towards all beings and it is not primarily meant for earning money or for fulfilling other desires.

In Vedic India and even later for many centuries, physicians were told that medical practice was never fruitless; it always gave some benefit or other for the doctor, not necessarily material or monetary. A Sanskrit-verse describes this idea as follows:

Sometimes puṇya, sometimes friendship,
Somewhere money, somewhere else fame,
Often knowledge and experience.
Never is treatment without its fruit.[1]

---

1. क्वचिद् धर्मं क्वचिद् मैत्री क्वचिद् वित्तं क्वचिद् यशः ।
क्वचिदर्थावबोधश्च चिकित्सा नास्ति निष्फला ॥

The aim and purpose of medical science was also very clearly defined: 'The "physician-ness" (the main characteristic) of a physician consists in understanding the nature of the disease and in relieving of distress. The physician is not the Lord of life.'[2] What a beautiful definition of the physician's duties and also his limitations! While emphasizing on great skill, the verse also teaches humility.

Thus in times gone by, high ideals were inculcated and, with the prevailing atmosphere of simple and dharmic living, the medical field was pervaded with ethical values. If at all anybody violated ethics—a rare occurrence—the local elders or the king took stringent action against the erring physician. The punishment was severe, as the physician is an educated person who should have been fully aware of all his duties and responsibilities.

Are these values observed or upheld today? Apparently not, as the recent years have witnessed a change in this scenario. Gradually there has grown an increasing tendency amongst doctors to adopt measures that are not always for the good of the patient. This has produced in the public mind a mistrust of the medical profession. Why has this happened? Is it due to the lack of emphasis on ethical values during the training of doctors, or due to the absence of a watchdog-institution that could guide and control doctors, or is it due to a general growth of Adharma that is being reflected in the medical profession and, if so, what can be done about it?

---

2. व्याधेः तत्त्वपरिज्ञानं वेदनायाश्च निग्रहः ।
एतद् वैद्यस्य वैद्यत्वम् न वैद्यः प्रभुरायुषः ॥

In recent years there has been a large and rapid increase in the number of medical colleges and the number of doctors in our country. Are they all of good standards? And are they all aware of ethical values in medicine? The application of the Consumer Protection Act to the medical profession has created a situation where it has become necessary to reexamine and reassert various facets of the problem of medical ethics. This has become important also because of the great technological progress that has been achieved in medical sciences, and which has increased the power of the medical profession over life and death. There are also factors like the changes in the ethical attitude of the society as a whole and the increasing level of general and medical knowledge amongst the public who want more information about their illnesses and their treatment.

The Medical Council of India is the authority to uphold ethics amongst medical practitioners. The Indian Medical Association is the premier and popular medical organization which is concerned with the highest quality of medical practice.

I would like to go back almost sixty years when as a young boy I asked my father, a general practitioner, why his name-board was smaller than the name-boards of the advocates and lawyers in the same street. His answer was that the ethics of the medical profession demanded that doctors should not advertise themselves, and if they do, they are likely to be censured by the Medical Council. Today such a discipline is absent amongst the members of the medical profession and one sees post-graduates attaching the designation of M.S. or M.D. to their names even when they are undergoing the course and the Medical Council appears powerless to prevent it.

Two major aspects have to be understood and discussed. One is the ethics of the medical profession in its regular day-to-day practice, with all the facets of doctor-patient relationship and doctor to doctor relationship. The other concerns specific major issues that have cropped up in recent decades like the issue of euthanasia, brain-death, abortions, transplantation, cloning, etc. The considered opinion of the leaders of the medical profession on these important issues must be placed before the public for their information and debate. It must be emphasized here that in these issues we in India should set standards in consonance with our culture and values, and not blindly follow the prejudices and limitations imposed by the Western culture.

While discussing the day-to-day practice of medicine in India, one finds that there are many factors that influence medical practice and the relationship of the doctors with their patients and the public.

An important recent development has been the technological leap that has occurred in methods of diagnosis and in the techniques of treatment. Conditions that were difficult to diagnose and impossible to treat two decades ago can all be tackled today with ease. This has placed an enormous responsibility on the shoulders of the modern doctor, who has to acquire the knowledge and the the skill commensurate with these advances, and also has to undertake more risky procedures than ever before. In the present day practice, the border-line between cure and risk to life has become narrow and situations often arise when the doctor has to weigh the balance very delicately. This places a great psychological burden on the profession and also requires the profession to keep itself updated on modern advances. If this is not insisted upon and practised by the medical profession, avoidable problems will result. The opportunity to achieve continuously the updated level of knowledge must be provided for the profession and there must be an insistence that the doctor must constantly be updating his or her knowledge and skills.

There are, of course, psychological limitations of both the physician and the patient. With the spread of education and scientific knowledge, people say that they have 'the right to know.' At the same time they seek from the medical profession solace and comfort and hope that their condition is not too serious and that they have a chance to recover. Often many patients assert that they are fully capable of withstanding any impact and demand to know every detail of their illness and the prognosis. But it is a rare human being who can face the full knowledge of a serious disease. How much should a doctor reveal and how much hope should he or she offer? How much does the principle of 'the right to know' conflict with the duty of the physician to offer comfort and hope? Will words of comfort be later on used against the doctor? This is a dilemma that places limitations on the doctors' willingness to do their best and take risks to save a life. This induces a psychological stress, which can be faced only by doctors with wide experience. How do we transfer this knowledge and experience to the younger generation of doctors?

There are limitations even at the entrance level to the medical courses. It is obvious that the chief motivation of young people today to enter the medical profession is the desire to earn money. The medical profession is seen by them and their parents and by the public as a safe and lucrative avenue of life. This is supported by the fact that parents are willing to pay large amounts of fees and donations or even adopt malpractices to get their sons and daughters into medical institutions. Because of this initial handicap, it is too much to expect the young doctors to be noble and altruistic. After all, they are also human. Apart from this, they have to contend with the fact that there is almost an absence of teaching about medical ethics and responsibility in the medical colleges. My generation learnt about medical ethics from our teachers by their example and we were often reminded of the ancient values of our profession.

But today's scene is different and good examples to follow may not be too many. Hence the Medical Council must insist on the teaching of medical ethics in the first, third and final years of undergraduate medical education and repeat a short course for all post-graduate trainees and continue reminding them of their ethical responsibilities.

Strangely, over the past two decades there has been in our country a swing towards materialism, a tendency opposed to our own culture of simplicity and dharma. Sociologists may attribute many reasons for these changes. But it is true that the milieu of society in which we live today provides little stimulus for nobility or altruism. At every turn the present generation of doctors meets with crass materialism, opportunism, and corruption from the lowest to the highest levels of society. The pursuit of wealth and material gain seems to be the sole aim that motivates society, and not the four values inherent in our culture, namely, Dharma, Artha, Kāma and Moksha.[3] To expect the medical profession alone to be pure milk in an ocean of salt water is unrealistic. Still, as the medical profession has to deal with the life and death of human beings, it has to raise itself to an acceptable level of ethics, so that the public will repose confidence in the profession.

The faith which our countrymen still have in the medical profession is almost unbelievable. A good good doctor is even now equated with God (*Vaidyo Narayaṇo Hariḥ*) and respected. Of course, there have been many situations when a different attitude was exhibited when medical help failed to achieve results, and the doctor was called the Lord of Death Yama's brother (*Yamarāja-sahodara*). But in general the faith placed by the Indian public in their doctors is moving. Sushruta says: 'The patient may doubt his mother and father, his sons, and his relatives, but he bestows his total faith in his physician's custody and never doubts about his sincerity. Therefore it is the physician's prime duty to look after the patient as his own child and with all affection.'

Such a faith should not be frittered away by a careless attitude on the part of the present younger generation. How this should be achieved is a matter of great concern.

When dealing with any profession, the concerned public would like to have an assurance that the members of the profession will always act ethically and with dignity and care, and at all times promote the interest of the patient. Such an assurance was provided for many centuries by

---

3. Artha (money) and kāma (enjoyment) are values, it is true, but we were taught in India to earn money in a way that did not conflict with dharma and to enjoy within the limits of one's earnings.

professional guilds as well as by the ruler himself. This was the system prevalent both in ancient India as well as in medieval England. In modern times, Medical Councils have been established in many countries and these have the responsibility of making sure that the members of the medical profession follow a code of ethics and always keep the interest of the patients foremost.

It is necessary to create afresh in the minds of people a strong confidence in the medical profession. This is not difficult, as so far only a few in the medical profession are tempted to act unethically. Teaching of medical ethics to undergraduates every alternate year of the medical courses, repeated refresher-courses in medical ethics for postgraduates and practitioners, and strengthening of the powers of the Medical Council with a will to act are the necessary immediate requirements.

Ethical or dharmic values are essential for the existence and for the progress of any society and have to be preserved and practised if human civilization has to progress. Of these values, ethics in medicine is of the greatest importance, as medicine deals with problems of life and death. To argue that the practice of values in medicine will depend on the condition of society is untenable, as the members of the medical profession belong to the élite in society and must shoulder greater responsibilities. They must have much greater concern about values than any other section of society. The doctor and the teacher—the Vaidya and the Upādhyāya—have to set a noble example to others in any civilized society.

23
Reflections on Suffering

Dr. William Pullen

That suffering and death are integral to human existence is clear. We are born, enjoy the brief illusion of immortality peculiar to youth, and reluctantly descend into an abyss of gradual deterioration punctuated by misery and culminating in death. This is our common material destiny. The occasional exceptions, spared the burdens of age, are mourned as dying before their time. However unpleasant life may be, it would seem, most prefer it to the alternative.

Man's suffering is the physician's charge. Bodily pain, intellectual anguish and spiritual despair keep us in business. The patient's calamity is the doctor's routine. As a Western physician whose philosophical foundation has been greatly influenced by Eastern thought, a number of observations occur.

One would think that death and dying should be a great impetus to spiritual evolution. However, much of modern Western culture has apparently evolved to distract us from our fate and at times even to conceal it from us. Medicine, once considered a healing art, is seen as a science whose purpose is to conquer disease and cheat death. The notion that nobility, or for that matter anything good, may arise from suffering has become passé. A treatment is expected, even demanded, for every complaint. And when finally life's end is reached, the process is hidden and the result sterilized.

Many in this country will find their last hours filled with fluorescent lights and unfamiliar faces. The desperate struggle to keep the body alive must seem, to the dying, like a final denial of their spiritual being. Loved ones, in simpler times, were often present to give comfort and bear witness. Such vigils must have helped many along their own spiritual paths. Not so now. Rather the terminally ill are often brought to the hospital by distraught family who bid the physician and all he commands to 'do everything possible.' By this, of course, they mean, keep the body alive. This process is often driven by guilt in the family, unreasonable expectations offered by physicians, and failure of the patient to have made contrary wishes known. Underlying this is the general lack of faith in any but a corporeal existence.

One final absurdity plays out after all measures to sustain life fail. The remains are cleverly hidden from view of the living until they can be whisked away, usually after dark, for their final attentions. The result is extraordinary. A carefully dressed and groomed body, preserved for all time, is returned to the family in a satin lined, hermetically sealed box. The eyes are closed, the expression placid, and the appearance that of stately repose. Grim evidence of the last agonal moments are replaced by the illusion of eternal slumber.

How is a physician to contend with such suffering? Despite our best efforts all our patients are destined to die, many miserably. The choices are few. Some can circumvent compassion and treat the whole matter as a scientific challenge. They may even argue that one's emotional responses cloud the clear reasoning needed to solve the problem at hand. However, most of us begin by caring deeply about our patients and inevitably have some emotional involvement. Over the years this takes a toll. Many are eroded by the endless presentations of suffering and the inevitable triumph of death. Seeds of despair are so sewn. The fruit, when ripe, has the bitter taste of cynicism.

My own professional life is sustained and often salvaged by my spiritual beliefs. The legacy of the body appears entirely unacceptable without the existence of the soul. If self-awareness, not Self-awareness, is truly the difference between man and beast, I should think we'd have all killed ourselves long ago. A properly planned suicide certainly seems preferable to an excruciating extinction. Nonetheless our species persists. An intuitive awareness of our true immortality is universal. This sense of immortality, when recognized as stemming from the soul, fosters spiritual growth and allows physical suffering to be experienced in a far more acceptable context. However, when the mind associates this same intuitive immortality with our material being, spiritual evolution is suppressed and bodily suffering becomes intolerable.

By recognizing the physical, intellectual and spiritual nature of human beings, a physician becomes more effective and less likely to slip into cynicism. Seeing the integration of body, mind and soul quickly leads to the conclusion that a disturbance in one inevitably affects the others. Treating the body without acknowledging the mind and soul fails to take proper advantage and often threatens harm.

Vedanta philosophy is particularly well suited to the practice of medicine. An irrefutable belief in the soul arises from our own spiritual experience. The resulting faith supports a vision of purpose and order that would be otherwise blinded by the daily spectacle of death and dying. Life's voyage through a seeming sea of suffering ceases to be tragic once the body is recognized as a vessel for the soul, not the sole vessel.

24

Values in Science and Technology

N. V. C. SWAMY

The word 'science' is derived from the Latin *scientia* meaning 'knowledge'. It thus represents the entire content of human knowledge. However, popular usage restricts it to the well-established natural sciences, viz., physical, chemical and biological sciences. Occasionally, mathematics is also included in this definition. It excludes all forms of knowledge which are intuitive in character and which cannot be explained by general laws.

Human knowledge about nature has been reached through a painstaking process of inquiry and discovery and innumerable errors. According to some diehard admirers of science, the acquisition and systematization of such knowledge is the only human activity that is truly cumulative and progressive. This point of view is not, of course, accepted universally. It is true that the triumphs of science represent a cumulative process of increasing knowledge and a sequence of victories over ignorance and superstition. It is also true that a stream of inventions has flowed from science for the improvement of human life. Nevertheless, there is now a better realization of deep moral problems within science, of external forces and constraints in its development, and of dangers in uncontrolled technological change. This has naturally led, in recent years, to a reappraisal of the value system governing science and technology, leading to a critical reassessment of their role in human life.

Value Systems in Science and Technology

The word 'value' is freely used in several contexts, but its meaning is somewhat vague. The dictionary meaning is 'that which is worthy of esteem for its own sake.' Books on moral philosophy define it as 'a belief that a specific mode of conduct or objective is personally or socially desirable.' According to St. Augustine, value is based on the will of God. Kant believes it to be based on reason aided by categorical imperatives. Hume feels that value judgments are based on human nature, sympathy or selfishness. Jeremy Bentham is of the opinion that it is based on the calculation of the greatest happiness of the greatest number. Even though these definitions differ from one another, there is a general common sense view that human values are a mixture of emotion, self-interest, reason, religious belief, and the experience of people in human society.

There is a mistaken impression among the non-scientific community that science is not concerned with values. But most people who are actively engaged in scientific research feel differently. Their experience is that scientific research is best done by a community which respects certain values. In his classic study of the sociology of science, Robert Merton enunciates four principal values, viz., universalism, communalism, disinterestedness, and organized scepticism.[1] These values are respected by scientists, not because they are personally more virtuous than non-scientists, but because if they do not obey them, their work will not be accepted and valued by the scientific community.

UNIVERSALISM. Universalism requires that science should be independent of race, colour or creed, and that it should be essentially international. In this sense, science is indeed a unifying factor among diverse races and creeds. It is rather unfortunate that the same cannot be said of religion and its practice. There is a specific reason for this. Any Tom, Dick and Harry who knows how to read and write can set himself up as an authority on religion. Most of the global conflicts based on religion can be traced to this cause. However, this is not possible in science. No scientist who claims to practise his profession can transgress this value of universalism, because he simply will not be acceptable to the community. There are no 'false prophets' in science.

Einstein is well-known as the discoverer of the Theory of Relativity. He enunciated the Special Theory in 1905 and followed it up with the General Theory in 1916. The latter

---

1. Merton, R. K., *The Sociology of Science* (Chicago University Press, 1973).

was confirmed by Sir Arthur Eddington in 1919 through his famous observations of the deflection of star-light by the gravitational field of the sun. Einstein became a celebrity overnight and was acknowledged all over the world as the true successor to Newton. However, this was the time when anti-Semitism was on the rise in Germany and Einstein was a Jew by birth. With the rise of Adolf Hitler to power, Einstein had to flee Germany to England, and later to USA. So much was the hatred of Hitler towards Jews that he dubbed the Relativity Theory as 'Jewish Science' and banned its teaching. He was supported in this mad venture by Phillip Lenard, who was himself a Nobel Prize winner in physics. This is one of the most sordid chapters in the history of twentieth century science. But this tirade of Hitler and Lenard could not find general acceptance with the scientific community, because of its deep-rooted commitment to the value of universalism.

Communalism. Communalism requires that scientific knowledge should be public knowledge. It also implies freedom of exchange of scientific information between scientists everywhere. It demands that scientists should be responsible to the scientific community for the trustworthiness of their published work.

The concept that the results of scientific research should be published for public knowledge started in Europe with the establishment of scientific academies like the Royal Society of London and the French Academy of Sciences in Paris. Since that time, it has become a tradition for all scientists to publish the results of their research in journals, whose numbers have now proliferated. The publication of any research work is not automatic. The paper communicated to a journal undergoes a rigorous peer review and is accepted for publication only when it satisfies the last requirement of communalism, i.e., the published work be trustworthy.

The Principia Mathematica, Newton's greatest achievement, was published in the year 1686. This contains the famous result about the application of his gravitational theory to the calculation of moon's orbit round the earth. Newton had completed this work almost twenty years earlier. Unfortunately, his calculations did not fully tally with available astronomical observations. Newton thought his theory was wrong and did not publish it. A crucial information needed for this calculation was the distance of the moon from the earth. He had used the value of this parameter based on the available records in the 1660s. More careful observations a couple of decades later showed that the earlier data was wrong. The more accurate value of moon's distance from the earth then became available to Newton. When he used this new value in his equation, he found a perfect agreement between his calculations and the observations. He then decided to incorporate his gravitational theory in the *Principia.* This is a typical illustration of the fidelity needed in scientific research.

Freedom of exchange of information between scientists is a sine qua non for the growth of science. That such an exchange is possible even in the midst of war is dramatically proved by the verification of Einstein's General Theory of Relativity. The epoch-making paper by Einstein was published in Germany in a German journal in the year 1916. Within a few months this came to the attention of Arthur Eddington in Cambridge, who started raising funds for an expedition to South America to verify the theory at the time of the solar eclipse predicted for 1919. This was the time when the First World War was at its most intense phase. Today, in retrospect, Eddington's project appears to have been foolhardy, but to Eddington, a true scientist, the war was irrelevant. For him the more important thing was Einstein's work. The verification of the General Theory by Eddington in 1919 firmly established its trustworthiness, leading to a revolutionary change in our concepts about the Universe.

Disinterestedness. This value requires that the results of bona fide scientific research should not be coloured or manipulated to serve considerations such as personal profit, ideology or expediency. In other words, they should be honest and objective. It is the impersonal nature of science which is its greatest strength.

The best example to show how science can get distorted if it is manipulated to suit an ideology is Soviet science during the communist regime. In its desire to prove the superiority of Communism over Capitalism, the Soviet regime forced the scientific community to claim that most of the important scientific advances made by the West had already been done in USSR much earlier. It was even claimed that the Theory of Relativity and Quantum Mechanics, which revolutionized human thought in this century, had already been discovered by Soviet scientists long before Einstein and Planck. The international community, however, could not swallow such a claim, because there was no proof available.

Many times it may so happen that different groups around the world may be working on the same research problem simultaneously. In such a situation, there often arises the question as to which group came up with the solution first. To resolve such conflicts, the scientific community has evolved a very efficient system. As soon as the results of a research work are communicated to a journal, the date of communication is registered. The paper is then sent to a set of referees, whose comments are essential to decide the quality of the work. If the paper is unconditionally accepted, it is published in the journal, indicating clearly the date on which it had been first communicated. In the event of the same results being published by different authors or different groups of authors, the date of communication is taken to establish priority. When C. V. Raman made his famous discovery leading to the Raman Effect in February 1928, he immediately wrote it up as a pamphlet, got it printed and rushed copies to all well-known scientists around the world. There were two more groups working on the same problem, one in France led by Cabannes, and the other in Russia led by Landsberg and Mandelstam. Since Raman publicized his results first, he was given the credit for the discovery and was awarded the Nobel Prize.

Plagiarism, or one scientist appropriating the work done by another scientist, is not uncommon in science. But because of free communication, the unwritten code of checks and balances is so effective that people just cannot afford to get away with plagiarism. This is one of the greatest strengths of science, that fraud gets detected easily and early, and also gets well publicized.

Organized Scepticism. This value requires that statements should not be accepted on the word of authority, but that scientists should be free to question them and that the truth of any statement should finally rest on a comparison with observed fact.

The most dramatic illustration of this is the case of S. Chandrasekhar, Indian-born Nobel Prize winner, who passed away in 1995. He is famous for his work on the behaviour of stars whose mass is greater than 1.4 times that of the sun. This is named after him as the Chandrasekhar Limit. He discovered his results when he was working in Cambridge, in 1930s, and showed them to Arthur Eddington, who had already earned world renown for his solar eclipse expedition to verify Einstein's General Theory of Relativity. Eddington was not convinced of Chandra's work and is reported to have said, 'Oh yes, your mathematics may be all right, but I don't think your physics is correct.'

Chandra decided to present his results in January 1935 at a meeting of the Royal Astronomical Society in London. According to the programme, Eddington was supposed to speak after Chandra. Chandra duly presented his results and was confident that the audience would appreciate his work. But to his horror Eddington, who followed him, ridiculed his work and cracked several jokes at his expense. Chandra was just a young Indian student and had no one to support him. He was deeply disappointed and left Cambridge once and for all for Chicago. Later observations and calculations, however, have vindicated Chandra and the scientific community honoured him profusely. But what is important to note is that even a great scientist like Eddington could not help his personal preferences intruding into his perception of work done by others.

After his epoch-making research in Relativity and Quantum Theory, Einstein became convinced that there exists a Grand Unified Theory which explains the whole universe. However, he was dismayed to note Schrödinger and Heisenberg introducing probabilistic concepts into Quantum Theory and made the famous statement: 'God does not play dice with the universe.' In spite of Einstein's objections and scepticism, it was the theory of Schrödinger and Heisenberg, who were still young novices, which gained acceptance, because they predicted and explained many new phenomena.

Innumerable are such instances in the history of science, where ideas have been accepted by the scientific community impartially, whether they came from a famous scientist or a novice. One of the greatest dangers faced by any society is credulousness and the antidote to this is a passion for the truth of fact. It is a precious yet vulnerable quality of the human spirit and science is its guardian.

Impact of Technology on the Value System

If we ask the man or the woman in the street what they think of science, what would their response be? About three centuries ago, at the time of Newton, most of them would have been unaware of what science is, except for a few who would have considered it as a pastime for the rich. About a hundred and fifty years ago, they would have acknowledged that science has made their lives more comfortable. They would have looked up to science to improve their material standard of living.

Today the answer would be completely different. The growth of science and its application to practical life in the form of technology have been so breathtakingly rapid in the current century that there is a sense of disquiet. Most people would regard science today as a mixed blessing. While there is a general feeling that science is a noble undertaking and necessary for the expansion of human knowledge, the same may not be said of technology.

Let us take another look at the values in science, enunciated in the earlier section, and see how they are viewed by technology. The value of universalism demands that knowledge be truly international. This is not true of technology. Today, thanks to the commercial exploitation of science and the related Intellectual Property Rights, technology has become the property of individuals or corporations. Consequently, it is no longer part of public knowledge, which is the basis of communalism. With the growth of Military Science and Defence Research, many technological developments have become classified and closed to the international community. This was particularly the situation during the era of the Cold War, when industrial and military espionage was at its highest. It was the personal experience of many of us in international conferences to meet Soviet scientists who could speak excellent English, but were accompanied by 'interpreters'!

Scientific research is no longer free of ideology, as witnessed, again, during the Cold War. The Russians launched the Sputnik and claimed that their science and technology was far superior to that of the Americans. Not to be left behind, the Americans landed a man on the moon claiming the supremacy of American science and technology. Even countries which cannot afford to provide food, clothing and shelter to their citizens are in a race to procure or develop bombs and missiles, because it is a matter of prestige for them to do so. The victim in this process is, of course, the value system on which science is based.

What about the cultural dimension of science? There is a general feeling among the public that science has dehumanized our view of the world. It is said that scientific thinking is 'mechanical' and not 'human' and has diverted the minds of people from spirituality and humanism. In the words of Sri Aurobindo, 'Even the discoveries of physical science have been elevated into a creed and in its name religion and spirituality banned as ignorance and superstition, philosophy as frippery and moonshine.'[2] Such accusations against science are not new. Even Newton feared that too wide an application of sciences would disenchant the world by reducing the need for God. The effect of such objections and accusations has been to make the public less friendly to science, to weaken the ideal of science as a vocation, and to put science on the defensive.

Are these criticisms justified? Part of the problem is that people often confuse science with technology. It is technology, emphasizing the material aspects of science, which is responsible for the concern expressed by thinkers like Sri Aurobindo. It is true that science and technology are distinct from each other, but it is hard to make that distinction in practice. There is a joke that if some major venture succeeds, it is called a 'triumph of science,' but if it fails, it is called 'failure of technology'!

---

2. Sri Aurobindo, *Essays on the Gita* (Pondicherry: Sri Aurobindo Ashram, 1989).

Value-based Science Education

Can something be done to remedy the situation? If it is a fact that most of the modern-day problems like pollution, global warming, ecological disasters, etc., have been due to the application of science, the remedy does not lie in discarding science altogether. The hope lies in solving these problems with the proper application of science. If the hole in the ozone-layer is caused by chlorofluorocarbons emitted by refrigerators and airconditioners, the solution does not lie in shutting down all such facilities, but in finding a substitute which is harmless.

To get more of what is desirable and less of what is undesirable, we must learn to control the applications of science embodied in new technologies. Many of the problems we are facing today—like nuclear waste disposal, toxic chemicals, misuse of genetic engineering, the import of new, unfamiliar and dangerous technologies by developing countries—are too complex to be tackled by passing legislative laws. If science and technology have created these problems, the two should be harnessed to provide solutions also.

It is here that education plays an important role. I am not referring here to school or college curriculum alone. We need to educate the public, the policy-makers, the bureaucrats, and even scientists, on the implications of new technologies. An open public debate many times brings greater cooperation from the various sections of society. The best example is the hazards of nuclear power. So long as the public is not properly educated about the pros and cons of nuclear power, there will always be a feeling of suspicion and fear. We are always more afraid of unknown dangers than known perils, the reason why we see ghosts in the dark and not in broad daylight. It is here that scientists have to play their part in demystifying science and bringing it with all its glory and faults to the man and the woman in the street.

The teaching of science in our schools and universities hardly achieves this purpose. According to John Ziman, '...the place of science in the popular culture of our time and the role of the scientist in contemporary society are largely determined by the way science is taught in the classroom. Although most people learn very little science, and make very little use of what they learn, they are the silent majority whose views eventually carry more weight than the tiny minority of research workers and advanced technologists. They too must learn something about science as part of their education about things in general.'[3] Of course, we cannot expect every 'educated' person to know much of actual, hard science as practised by scientists. But it is desirable that every 'educated' person should know more *about* science.

The key to a peaceful and happy existence on this mysterious planet is a better understanding of ourselves and the world around us. We know more about ourselves and the world than any society has ever known before, thanks to modern science. If we have to use this knowledge wisely, we need to treat science as an integral and valuable part of our culture and not simply as an agent of material progress. We need to respect and cherish the value system that has made science such a thrilling adventure.

---

3. Ziman, John, *Teaching and Learning about Science and Society* (Cambridge: University Press, 1980).

25

Values in Industry

K. C. SHROFF

At Excel we say, 'Industry is the manifestation of excellence in people'—excellence of body, mind, and soul.

The Excel Industries started in a kitchen in 1941 and it got all its value system from the mother's kitchen. The values like service, accuracy, and consistency. The urge for innovativeness, thrift, versatility, and team work. Energetic cooperation (*saha vīryam*), our Vedic heritage.

Since more than half a century, the Company has been growing and, from an initial investment of Rs.10,000, its assets now touch Rs.1000 million, with a turnover of more than Rs.2500 million, export-earnings touching Rs.400 million. The Company operates from five manufacturing sites, half a dozen zonal offices, and more than 15,000 distribution points.

Every Excelite is a shareholder in the Company. Sometimes three generations of the family have worked in the Company.

From the beginning we at the Excel knew that any industry survives because of the customer. Profit is the by-product of the services given. In order to maintain good profits one has to be innovative, because needs change and customers also change. One has always to be on the lookout for new, easily available raw materials and convert them into much-needed products for the market.

If I repeat about the excellence of the body, mind and soul, it is just to emphasize that good industry does not sustain on the strength of money or machine but on the quality of its personnel.

We are often asked the question, everywhere there is so much corruption, substandard work, unethical practices, yet how do you manage to grow? From where do you get excellent people to continually expand your activities? I would like to share our experience on this subject.

Swami Vivekananda said that education is the manifestation of the perfection already present in us. He said that our present-day education system is capable of producing only clerks. He demanded the starting of centres where man-making, character-building education would be imparted. For this type of education we need to instil in students faith (*śraddhā*) and concentration (*ekāgratā*), and help them build up the sense of nonduality (*advaita*) and harmony (*samanvaya*).

As we went on studying this message of Swamiji, we realised that only a good industry could become the school of Swamiji's dream. An industry has to be the new Gurukula. The seniors in an industry are the acharyas, teachers and performers, and they have to get the next in line, their juniors, ready to take up their responsibility in a phased manner. It is only in an industry that real energetic cooperation (*saha vīryam*) becomes possible.

People interrelate with each other to achieve results. No individual or his/her function is complete in itself. It is only the sum total of all activities that creates completeness and brings full results. So every worker in an industry has to interact with others and that is why we are able to see the manifestation of perfection in others all the while.

We realise that our own industry also is not complete in itself. We all are interrelated and interdependent. There are the suppliers, there are the finance agencies and, of course, there are the customers. All are trying to manifest their perfection in their own way. We must recognize this truth.

Now we all realize so well that yesterday's know-how gets outdated today and we have to learn and interrelate continually with others to keep in step with new trends and inventions. We can easily understand today that only the teachings of Swami Vivekananda can keep us effective, useful, and ahead of our times.

Every person working in an industry must love and respect every other coworker. This love, respect and togetherness can best be expressed by eating together. At Excel Industries we always eat together—same food, same place, same utensils, and same discipline. We have no hierarchy in the dining hall.

Through such relationship and creative interaction, the Excel Industries produced on a commercial scale more than a hundred different products, most of them for the first time in India.

When we look ahead to the twenty-first century and further, we have a choice to make. We can either continue the present Western exploitative way of management and end up as a highly polluted, scarcity-prone and strife-ridden urbanized society, or we can have a fresh understanding of our heritage, our eternal values, and our rich natural resources. Sunlight, warm air, rain water, soil and the innumerable products emerging out of it are useful to all living beings. Nature has her own way of maintaining the ecological balance. It is we greedy humans who put obstacles in her path. We must remember that the balance will remain intact so long as we live by our Vedantic values, respecting the whole creation, and seeing it as the manifestation of the Divine (*īśā vāsyam idam sarvam*).

We human beings are a small insignificant part of the universe and yet we are powerful enough to damage the environment and to self-destruct. Much damage has already been done, but the situation is not yet hopeless. We can still turn the tide. The question is, Have we learnt the lessons so essential for the future well-being of our planet and its occupants? Rest assured the earth is not going to perish, but the human race *can* perish unless we reexamine our values and remove the aberrations from our individual and collective lives.

This is where the teachings of Swami Vivekananda come to our rescue and give us hope and the courage to persevere. These are the lessons we have learnt at the Excel Industries.

26

Values in Business

DOUG RAUCH

There has been a long history of philosophical debate as to the complex nature of value, or ethics, as well as the validity of business or its purpose in society. Other than to clarify some terms, that debate is not the scope of this article. Far greater minds, both religious and secular, have explored these issues in depth. Instead, let's explore the applications of Vedanta, especially as it relates to the modern business experience. Let's look at what the attempt to bring values, particularly spiritual values, to business means today.

Before we can even begin to discuss this subject, we have to clarify what is meant by business. For the purposes of this article, 'business' will be defined broadly. Business not only refers to the organization or institution engaging in trade, but also to the act of engaging in that profession. Business can be for profit or not-for-profit. It can employ thousands or encompass the self-employed. Business involves all actions related to one's occupation or profession, whether that be as a retail merchant, teacher, or monastic.

There are some who have the general feeling that the very subject of 'business ethics' or values is an oxymoron, like 'hot ice.' Indeed, the world, including the business world, can appear to be a harsh desert for those attempting to lead a spiritual life. The tendency in business, just as in the world, often appears as selfishness, as a pull toward separateness, toward *avidyā māyā*.

However, our experience in business should not be fundamentally different from the rest of our life. Our life is an integrated whole, not separate compartments. We can't spend our time at work in a way that is harmful to our spiritual values and expect to grow spiritually. The mind, wherein our thoughts and actions make their impressions, is the same at work as it is at home. The thoughts and actions we undertake at work become a part of us at home also. This is the fundamental reason why we can't have two codes of values that are in conflict: 'business ethics' for work and 'personal ethics' for home.

We must find a way to lead our business life in harmony with our inner life. All sincere spiritual aspirants struggle with integrating their inner life with their outward actions. This is the universal struggle we all experience. Without finding a place of balance, a harmony between the 'spiritual' and the 'secular', or the outer and the inner, we will experience frustration and discouragement.

Based upon this frustration, some see business as a necessary evil. Necessary to provide income, but little more. It is to be endured, not embraced. However, since most of us aren't called to the completely contemplative life, we have to engage in some form of business. This being the case, we'd better find a way to minimize the negative effects of work, or perhaps to turn our business endeavours into a spiritual aid. Business, like work in general, is in itself neither good nor bad (or, from a relative point of view, business can be good or bad depending upon what we make it). How we engage in business and our intentions in doing so are what will determine its impact on our life.

As Krishna stated in the *Gita,* all of us must perform action, our very nature will force us into action. None of us can escape work. So the question, as it applies to business, is which values will turn work into an aid to our spiritual growth.

But let's clarify what we mean by values. Let's look at the basic meaning as given in a dictionary: 'Value is that quality of anything which renders it desirable or useful.'[1] In this light let's look at which values in business would render it useful for spiritual growth. Here the philosophy of Vedanta has much to offer the spiritual aspirant. Vedanta offers a perspective that nurtures values conducive to business. Each of these values needs to be complementary to one's inner practice.

Unity in Variety. This seems to be the basis for all ethics and values, in business as well as our individual lives. It is the belief in the interconnectedness of all life

1. *Random House Dictionary of the English Language,* 2d edn. (New York, 1987), 2103.

that creates the golden rule, or the value of business ethics. One of the key corollaries is that there are no 'situational business ethics.' You can't have one set of rules for business, and another for your personal life. There is one set of values or ethics for all individuals. There is no 'class' structure in ethics.

As this applies to business, if you attempt to achieve personal gain by another's loss, you will find yourself poorer. Perhaps it won't be apparent at first, for financially you may seem to succeed, but in the long run you will be sowing the seeds of failure. By recognizing and acting on unity we can celebrate the variety of life. In business this means we don't have to fear differences in others, but can embrace the fascinating variety of life.

Win / Win. Related to the belief in the unity of existence is the goal to create business relations that are 'win/win'. These are mutually beneficial relationships where both parties gain in an atmosphere of free choice and mutual respect. As we grow and evolve, we recognize that there are several levels of business interaction. The lowest I'd call Exploitation (or Win/Lose). This is where one seeks gain at any cost to others. The end justifies the means; values are ignored. This is the business equivalent of the brute or bully. The next level is Competition. This is where the majority of business and individuals live today. The focus is internal: on the business or the self, not on the big picture. Whether an interaction is beneficial to another is not a concern. This is the business equivalent of egotistical behaviour: the gains to oneself may appear to be real, but it is based upon the ephemeral nature of all things. Developing the value of 'win/win', the only interactions or relationships an individual would welcome in a business environment would be mutually beneficial.

Karma Yoga. One of the foremost values in business is the ability to approach work as selfless service or worship, called karma yoga. Business can become karma yoga (instead of just busy-ness) when we are engaged in selfless action without regard to the results. This has immense ramifications in business. To the degree that we can practise karma yoga we experience freedom from anxiety over the effects of our actions; freedom from the cravings of ambition. Without becoming overly attached to the results of our actions we can work without fear, focusing on the job in front of us. We can live in the present moment. As a result we can give our best effort to the job at hand, not letting worry or longing distract us. Karma yoga also teaches us that motive is as important as action. We must strive to have the right intentions as well as the right actions.

Service. All of the really successful companies have established their success on the bedrock of customer service. This value is easily spiritualized into serving the highest aspect in man: seeing the customer as a manifestation of the Divine. Of course, following Ramakrishna's advice, we should be devotees, not fools. We should use all our abilities to engage in service that treats us as well as our customers respectfully. There is nothing spiritual in a 'lose/win' relationship. This is the business equivalent of self-abuse.

Work as Play. Vedanta allows us to maintain perspective: to see the big picture—it's all the eternal play of the Self. From this point of view, challenge is now embraced instead of feared. As the Self, what is there to fear? Of course, few of us can maintain this attitude but, to paraphrase the *Gita,* 'even a little knowledge of yoga relieves one of great fear.' We can work with a real sense of cheerfulness, knowing that the results of the 'game' are not in our hands.

Higher Purpose. Business is not the be-all and end-all of life. With a higher goal in life we experience a deeper sense of meaning and purpose. It becomes much easier to keep our sense of balance at work when we have a higher purpose that transcends all business endeavours. And with this value, it is much easier to resist the temptations to let the end justify the means in any business decision.

Surrender/Patience. Related to karma yoga, surrender is a key value in business. You must recognize when you are 'pushing on a string'—when something just isn't going to happen. Whether this be a promotion or the hope of getting a new customer, the ability to 'let go, let God' is a valuable tool. It is also by surrender that we learn to keep our ego out of our way. Anyone on the spiritual path must develop patience and perseverance (or they will become immensely frustrated indeed!). These two values become essential in any business endeavour.

Openness. When you can surrender, you allow yourself to become open to new possibilities. It is the stance of openness in business that often allows a new way of looking at something to occur. It encourages a flow of creativity in yourself and others—particularly when you share an attitude of openness with your business associates. This also reinforces the ability to celebrate variety: when you are open to others, you are tolerant and accepting. In business these values gain you respect even among your noble competitors.

Reflection. Business provides the opportunity to complement one's personal meditation practice. By focusing on the work at hand, practising concentration and mental discipline at work, the mind is less likely to wander when you ask it to sit quietly at home. Of course, this assumes that your work environment is not too full of distractions and negative input.

Business as the Health Club of Spirituality. As far fetched as this may seem, business forces each of us to exercise our spiritual values in an environment that resists such efforts. It is in the arena of work that most of us come to grips with our real level of spiritual unfoldment: this is where 'the rubber meets the road.' It is easy to talk about detachment or seeing God in all, but when we are pressed into action, we discover our shortcomings. As long as we don't give up, we should be thankful that there is an arena that provides us the opportunity, indeed may even challenge us, to exercise our spiritual values.

Vedanta provides a worldview that embraces both the spiritual and the physical in a vision of unity. It provides a synthesis to the conflict between business and spirituality. If we look at business as an arena to develop the values necessary for spiritual practice we find that the opportunities to give work a spiritual turn are unlimited. Business then provides a chance to express one's deepest convictions and experiences as a form of service and worship—whether of a Personal God or the underlying unity of existence.

27
Values in Sport

R. MOHAN

What role does sport play in society? A case can be made for a demeaning, even damaging role. Games always hinge on winning and losing, and aesthetics are a secondary consideration. Sport, seen by some as surrogate war, breeds aggression. Such a case is, however, only caricature in which the least attractive parts of sport are seen for the whole.

Sport, despite its history which began in Olympia almost three millenniums ago, has been undervalued by intellectuals and social historians. It does not hold anymore the hallowed place the Greeks reserved for it. Organized sport had been a part and parcel of the civilization of Ancient Greece. When that civilization crumbled, sport went down with it and there was to be no organized sport in Europe for another 1500 years.

In Greece, the athletes were fêted by the public. They were given jobs, generally to run the local gymnasium, and were fed and housed at the village or city expense. It was the public which could afford to underwrite the games by paying for the individual athlete's participation. The laurels they earned were held in great esteem.

Let us take a look at the scene today. Mike Tyson, the world class boxer with some claim to all-time star status in the sport, has just served time in jail after being convicted of rape. The former Americal gridiron footballer O. J. Simpson was on trial for the murder of his wife and her friend, and until he was acquitted, it was a trial which held America in thrall.

Values? Did not sport inculcate any values at all in these men? Look around the world of sport today and it is filled with as much corruption and sleaze as it is financially rewarding for those who excel in it. There is little reason to doubt that money has been the single biggest corrupting factor. When mammom beckons, morality takes a back seat.

A Test captain has been stood down for suspected fixing of international matches in collusion with bookmakers after visiting cricketers accused him of offering them bribes to under-perform. The football circuit in the Far East has been shattered by similar betting and bribery scandals. So much so, they are asking all the players and officials to declare their assets.

By no means is such fraud or fear of it a modern phenomenon. History is rife with the mean acts of sportsmen who have sold their integrity for a few dollars more.

Such acts did not have to face the scrutiny as they do in the glare of the harsh media spotlight of today. Betting on sport is as old as the hills. But throwing matches in collusion with certain undesirable forces is by far the more heinous crime. It is unfortunately true that the brightest of sportsmen have done this to make a quick buck.

The case for the prosecution rests. Corruption is commonplace in sport of the postmodern age. Let us take up the defence case now, lest you have already come to believe that this is the most negative sporting article you have ever read.

Sport has for long triggered an unforced sense of community. When Kapil Dev captured the world Test bowling record with wicket number 432, we as a nation rejoiced. It was as if the universal had merged in an individual. His aspirations, his achievement, his joy were shared by millions and millions of people. This is what sport does to people, to nations.

Sport is an ennobling concept even if its practices have been corrupted through the ages by being buffeted by social and political forces. It has bred in us values which have remained unaltered, pristine. How many times have we told ourselves that we will not appeal if we do not believe the batsmen is out? Times without number we have applauded a good stroke from the opposing batsmen.

Sorry about my bias for cricket. But since I have been bred in its values, I only present them as examples of what sport has done to enrich our lives by being the very medium which has shaped it. Cricket's role in forming values and character has long been appreciated. In fact, it is a way of life in the Commonwealth to say of anything that is underhand—'It's not Cricket.'

In the case for the prosecution, the severe examples of Tyson and Simpson were held out. In the case for the defence are the examples of millions of others who have benefited from the values that sports, just any game, be it a bruising physical contact sport or one with greater aesthetic values like cricket, have inculcated in them.

At a very basic level sport teaches the individual to subjugate his selfish interests to those of the team. Personal inclinations and interests have to be subordinated to the good of the whole. A sense of fraternity becomes strong through sporting contact. How often we remember even those sportsmen whom we played against in our school and college days!

I quote the Marxist historian and cricket writer par excellence, C. L. R. James of Trinidad, to make the point about how sport elevates: 'We kept a stiff upper lip in that we did not complain about ill-fortune. We did not denounce failures but "Well tried" or "Hard luck" came easily to our lips. We were generous to opponents and congratulated them on victories even if we knew they did not deserve it. We lived in two worlds. Inside the classrooms the heterogeneous jumble of Trinidad was battered and jostled and broken down into some sort of order. On the playing field we did what ought to be done.'

I find that line most significant when James says, on the playing field they did what ought to be done. There is a sense of fair play which sport breeds so easily. The unwritten code learnt on the playing fields of a school or college more often serves a man well in life more than many textbooks which describe the lives of great people.

Why do we spend so much time on sports which some may see as childish pursuits? If sport were not a microcosm of life in which we learn so much, we would not have spent on it so much energy and time in the last hundred and fifty years in which sport has got back its organized moorings.

Sport has now received a hallowed place in society, thanks to the recognition of its contribution. It is not only the entertainment that sports hold out to the populace which has given it such an exalted place in the present day. The proliferation of television has had much to do with spreading a message.

The spread of television and the live coverage of major sporting events and the revenues that are generated have brought to bear even greater responsibilities on sportsmen. As they play and compete often in front of a global audience, which has access to such quality pictures from the candid cameras of television, sportsmen have perforce to be models of sportsmanship.

History will record the contribution of the television medium. Live coverage has been the single biggest innovation of the modern age and its spread promises to clean up much of sport. An audience in excess of a billion, not unknown for such fixtures as the football World Cup final, bring sport into such focus as to place a premium on correct behaviour.

So what about sports federations appointing referees and match commissioners with sweeping powers to fine players for misbehaviour? The necessity for such a corrective mechanism is not to be understated. It is a sign of the times that players have to be reprimanded or fined in order to ensure their total compliance not only with the letter of the law but also its spirit as well as the spirit behind the code of conduct.

What sport has done is to give us a code for life itself. In laying down a code of ethics and in giving us a set of values, sport has been instrumental in shaping our lives in some way. It is only intellectual snobbery or sheer ignorance which prevents people from recognizing what role sport has played and will continue to play in society.

It does appear as if the case for the defence is stronger than the case for the prosecution. The honourable judge would be well advised to base his judgment on the positive contribution of sport to humanity and its place in history and in society. The judge might just be inclined to advise all that they must stick to the values that the tradition of sports has given us.

Contributors

Swami Bhajanananda, a former editor of the *Prabuddha Bharata*, is a senior monk of the Ramakrishna Order. He is an Assistant Secretary of the Ramakrishna Math and the Ramakrishna Mission, and lives at the Order's headquarters in Belur Math.

His Holiness the Dalai Lama was educated in the Tibetan traditions to prepare for a role that embodied the highest spiritual and temporal authority in Tibet. In 1950 at the age of 16 he was called upon to assume full political authority as the country faced the Chinese invasion. Since 1959 the Dalai Lama has been living in India, where he runs a government in exile, working to preserve the Tibetan identity and to place the issue of Tibet on the international agenda. His philosophy of altruism, compassion, nonviolence, and peace have made him a statesman who is greatly respected, admired and loved all over the world. The Dalai Lama was honoured with the Nobel Peace Prize in the year 1989.

Pravrajika Vrajaprana, of Cree descent, is a nun of the Vedanta Society of Southern California at Sarada Convent, Santa Barbara, USA. She is the author of *My Faithful Goodwin* (Advaita Ashrama, 1992) and editor of *Living Wisdom: Vedanta in the West* (Vedanta Press, 1994 and Madras Math, 1996). Her biography of Sister Christine, titled *Sister Christine: A Portrait,* is due for release soon.

SWAMI VIDYATMANANDA is a senior monk of the Ramakrishna Order. Editor in an American publishing house for several years before he joined the monastery at the Vedanta Society of Southern California, he thereafter wrote, compiled and edited many books which have enriched Vedanta literature. In 1966 the Swami shifted to the Order's ashrama in France, where he now stays.

NIVEDITA R. BHIDE is an All-India Secretary for the educational activities of the Vivekananda Kendra, Kanyakumari. She joined Vivekananda Kendra, a spiritually oriented service mission, in 1977. Since then she has worked in the Kendra's Rural Development Project and was the Principal of the high school at Vivekanandapuram, Kanyakumari, before taking her present charge as an All-India Secretary.

HEDI AND NIK BOESTEN of Kiel, Germany, are devotees and members of the Centre Vedantique Ramakrichna, Gretz, France.

AASHA REDDY is a devotee closely associated with Sri Ramakrishna Math, Madras.

SWAMI GAUTAMANANDA, a senior monk of the Ramakrishna Order, is the head of Sri Ramakrishna Math, Madras. He is also a trustee of the Ramakrishna Math and a member of the Governing Body of the Ramakrishna Mission.

PIERRETTE MOHAN, a member of the Centre Vedantique Ramakrichna, is an educational counsellor in a school in France.

D. K. OZA, M.A. (Gandhian Thought), I.A.S. (Retd.), was an Administrative Officer in Tamil Nadu from 1957 to 1990. He is currently Project Advisor to the Kasturba Gandhi National

Memorial Trust. A Fulbright Scholar 1992, Mr. Oza is the author of *Voluntary Action and Gandhian Approach: A Study of Three Voluntary Movements in India* (1991), which has been translated into four Indian languages.

Charles Kingman Mitchell holds a Masters Degree in American Literature from Indiana University and the Juris Doctor degree from Southwestern University School of Law. He has been a university lecturer and instructor in American literature and philosophy, and was for several years director of the First Liberty Church in Santa Monica, California. He is presently general counsel to the Vedanta Society of Southern California and a vice president of its board of trustees. Mr. Mitchell has his law offices in Marina Del Rey, California, USA.

Nani A. Palkhivala, eminent constitutional lawyer and an authority on tax laws, is the author of *The Law and Practice of Income Tax, Our Constitution Defaced and Defiled,* and *We the People,* besides many other books. A champion of free speech and unfettered press, Mr. Palkhivala has successfully argued a number of historic cases in the courts of India and abroad. He was India's ambassador to USA from 1977 to 1979.

Julio Francis Ribeiro joined the Indian Police Service in 1953. After serving in various capacities in Bombay and in various districts of Maharashtra, he was appointed Director General (D.G.) of Central Reserve Police Force (CRPF), and later, D.G. of Police in Gujarat. His tenure as D.G. of Punjab Police from 1986 to 1988 is most remembered for the efficiency and firmness with which he brought under control the menace of terrorism. Mr. Ribeiro was later India's ambassador to Romania for four years (1989–93). He was awarded the Indian Police Medal for Meritorious Service in 1972, President's Police Medal for Distinguished Service in 1978, and the Padma Bhushan in 1987.

Pravrajika Varadaprana, a senior nun of Vedanta Society of Southern California at Sarada Convent, Santa Barbara, USA, is well-known in the Western Vedanta Movement as a musician and composer. The texts she sets to music include verses from the Bhagavad Gita, Vedic peace chants, and songs from *The Gospel of Sri Ramakrishna.* Two cassette recordings that have been made of her compositions are: 'Filled with Brahman' and 'We Are One.'

Swami Veetamohananda, a senior monk of the Ramakrishna Order, is the head of Centre Vedantique Ramakrichna, Gretz, France.

Rajkumar Bharathi is a young and versatile musician trained in both Hindusthani and Carnatic classical music by renowned Masters. He is a great-grandson of the famous poet-revolutionary Subramanya Bharathi. Rajkumar has given music concerts all over India and in many countries abroad. He has also sung for films and composed music for ballets. He has several music-cassettes to his credit, including a 4-volume set of the entire *Bhagavad Gita* (produced by Sri Ramakrishna Math, Madras).

Alan Arkin, of New York, is actor, director, and writer. His over 40 films as an actor include *The Russians Are Coming, Popi, The Heart Is a Lonely Hunter, The In-Laws, The Rocketeer, Edward Scissorhands,* and *Glengarry Glen Ross.* He directed the film *Little Murders* along with many plays for the stage and programmes for television. He is the author of *Halfway Through the Door*, and of several books for children.

Guy E. Olson was until September 1995 editor of *SPAN*, a monthly published by the U.S. Information Service in India. Previously he edited USIS magazines for the Arab world, the former Soviet Union, and several East European countries. He began his journalism career 25 years ago as a staff correspondent for United Press International in the United States. Mr. Olson now has a new assignment with the U.S. Information Agency in Washington.

Jean-Marc Ohlmann, of Paris, France, is a trained journalist. He has worked for press, radio, and TV, and has now switched over to writing novels and screenplays.

Ann Louise Bardach is a contributing editor to *Vanity Fair* and also writes for *The New Republic.* In 1995 she received the PEN West award for journalism.

Barbara Dana, of New York, is a children's book author, screenwriter, and actress. Her books include *Young Joan, Necessary Parties, Zucchini, Zucchini Out West,* and *Rutgers and the Water-snouts.* Among her screenplays are *Necessary Parties* and *Arigo.* Barbara Dana has acted in many plays, in films, and on television.

B. Ramamurthi, M.S., F.R.C.S., F.A.C.S., F.I.C.S., F.A.M.S., F.A.Sc., F.N.A.Sc., F.N.A., is a leading neurosurgeon in India today. He has worked against great odds to establish neurosurgery on a firm basis in the country, set up postgraduate training in neurosciences, and helped to create many departments of neurosurgery all over India. He has held important positions in many international and national Scientific Societies.

For his contribution to neurosurgery in the Indian armed forces, Dr. Ramamurthi has been made an honorary Brigadier, and his services to the country were recognized by the President of India by honouring him with the title Padmabhushan.

WILLIAM PULLEN, M.D., is a practising physician in Santa Monica, California, USA. He is a Clinical Assistant Professor of Medicine at the University of California at Los Angeles and long time member of the Vedanta Society of Southern California.

N. V. C. SWAMY, B.E., M.Sc., Ph.D., was, until his retirement in December 1995, Director of the Indian Institute of Technology, Madras, and Professor in its Department of Applied Mechanics. A Fellow of the National Academy of Engineering, he has travelled widely in India and abroad. Eighty-nine of Prof. Swamy's research papers have been published in national and international journals and conference-proceedings.

KANTISEN C. SHROFF is a cofounder, with his elder brother, of Excel Industries Limited, Bombay, a prestigious chemical industry with a product range of over 20 chemicals. Mr. Shroff is actively engaged with Vivekananda Research and Training Institute, which does rural development work in the drought-prone areas of Kutch (Gujarat), including activities like cattle care, social forestry, watershed management, and employment generation.

DOUG RAUCH is the President of one of the fastest growing retail companies in America. He has received his Executive Masters in Business Administration at the Drucker School of Management. He has been practising Vedanta for over twenty-five years.

R. Mohan, Cricket Correspondent of *The Hindu* and *The Sportstar*, has reported over 100 Test matches and over 300 one-day internationals in a journalistic career of 20 years. The most widely travelled of Indian sports writers, he has managed to be close to the players while also being forthright in his comments on their cricket. Mohan has coauthored a book on Kapil Dev, titled *Cricket: My Style*, and has collaborated with him in his new book, *Triumph of the Spirit*.

Swami Tyagananda is a monk of the Ramakrishna Order. The Introduction to this book appeared originally as an editorial in the *Vedanta Kesari*.